STAND OUT

Other Books for Teens by Bill Sanders

Life, Sex, and Everything in Between
Outtakes: Devotions for Girls
Outtakes: Devotions for Guys
Goalposts: Devotions for Girls
Goalposts: Devotions for Guys
Tough Turf: A Teen Survival Manual
Stand Tall: Learning How to Really Love Yourself
Stand Up: Making Peer Pressure Work for You

STAND OUT

How You Can Become a Strong Leader

BILL SANDERS

Fleming H. Revell
A Division of Baker Book House
Grand Rapids, Michigan 49516

Published by Fleming H. Revell
a division of Baker Book House Company
P.O. Box 6287, Grand Rapids, MI 49516-6287

Printed in the United States of America

Library of Congress Cataloging-in-Publication Data

Sanders, Bill, 1951–
    Stand out : How you can become a strong leader / Bill Sanders.
       p.   cm.
    ISBN 0-8007-5533-2
    1. Leadership—Juvenile literature. 2. Leadership—Moral and
ethical aspects—Juvenile literature. 3. Leadership—Religious
aspects—Christianity—Juvenile literature. 4. Youth—Conduct of
life—Juvenile literature. [1. Leadership. 2. Conduct of life.] I.
Title.
HM141.S26   1994
303.3'4—dc20   94-28907

Unless otherwise noted Scripture quotations are taken from *The Living Bible,*
copyright © 1971 by Tyndale House Publishers, Wheaton, Illinois. Used by
permission.

Contents

Who's a Leader?

What would cause an entire football team to have so much compassion and love for a fellow student who had lost his hair to leukemia that they would shave their heads so he wouldn't feel alone and out of place? They could have fought the other students who were calling their friend names like cue ball, baldy, and onion head, but instead they decided to STAND OUT and live the Golden Rule.

Why would one junior high girl have the courage to sit next to the most feared and despised bully the school had ever known? Why would she become his friend when no one else would have anything to do with him? Why would she want to STAND OUT from her friends and be nice to the guy that beat up her brother the day before?

How could a guy with no right hand make the high school, college, and major league teams as a pitcher and against all odds throw a no-hitter for the New York

Yankees? With less natural ability than hundreds of previous big league pitchers and only half the required number of hands, what kind of determination, drive, and desire caused this likable young man to STAND OUT from so many others striving for this most cherished and elusive goal?

Why would one of the most famous speakers of all time invite dozens of other speakers to his organization to give away his secrets on how to reach teens? And to top that, why would he personally help the speakers get to their rooms by carrying their bags? When I asked him why he seemed so full of pleasure in serving us, he said: "My hero washed feet." He was willing to STAND OUT and be a servant.

How could a woman who had just left her husband's funeral go to the house of the teenage boy who had accidentally hit him with his car and tell him that God was in control and that he should forgive himself so his life wouldn't be ruined? What special stuff did she possess inside that would cause her to STAND OUT from other angry and resentful people and give an innocent young man the freedom to live?

What would cause professional athletes to say no to the pressures of premarital sex in an age when "everybody who is anybody is doing it" and to start an organization called "Athletes for Abstinence"? With plenty of available females at every turn and so many other sports stars taking advantage of them, what causes some superstars to STAND OUT and stick to their morals?

What would drive a sixth-grader to STAND OUT from all his other classmates and gather enough signatures to encourage the state of Ohio to adopt its new motto: All things are possible with God?

Why would a nun give up fame and fortune to serve this world's downtrodden? When her picture gets on the cover of nationally-known magazines and they tell her inspiring stories, what causes her to STAND OUT from the crowd and give all the glory to God?

Being a leader who STANDS OUT from the complacent crowd is what this book is all about. The secrets of the people you have just read about and dozens more are awaiting you in the pages ahead. You'll learn how to become the type of person you will be proud to look at in the mirror. I'm talking about real, live, hard-to-find, positive leadership—the stuff heroes are made of. I want you to become the kind of leader you don't read much about anymore—not a manipulative, self-serving, dictator-type leader, but the kind of leader we all admire.

The world is ready for *you* and all that *you* have to offer. You have what it takes! I know that without even knowing you. I can say that with confidence because I've been studying leaders for over twenty years. They come in all shapes, sizes, and backgrounds. God made you and he makes no mistakes. By following the step-by-step techniques in this book you can (and *will!*) better yourself and find that you can fulfill the unique dreams that God has given to you.

I answer over two thousand letters each year from people of all ages, especially teens, who are trying desperately to figure out what makes some people successful and some people miserable for their entire lives. *Stand Out* is filled with simple yet seldom-used principles that can help you be the kind of integrity-filled person our world is trying so hard to find. All you have to do is learn the principles and apply them. In order to do that you must read on and put into practice what you learn. STAND OUT and make it happen!

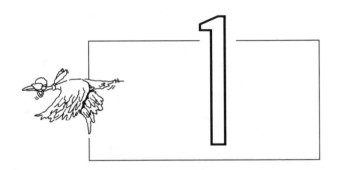

Leadership!
What's That?

"Sure, being famous means you're a leader," Rick contended when he talked about the subject with his best friend. "After all, leaders always hit the evening news, don't they?"

"No way," Paul objected. "Lots of people in the news couldn't lead their way out of a paper bag."

Just as Rick and Paul had different understandings of the relationship between leading and fame, most people don't have a clear view of the issue. Have you ever asked yourself what a leader is? Do you know how to become a good leader?

Leadership Quiz

Ask yourself the following questions.

How much do fame and popularity have to do with
  leadership?

Don't leaders all have "the good life" at their fingertips?

Can you be famous and not be a leader?

Can you be a leader and not be famous?

Fame, Leadership, and All That

I asked Beth to name someone famous—a real
superstar.

"Madonna," Beth said, right off the top of her head.
"She's famous all right—you'll see her face in all the
magazines and see her on TV."

"Do you think she's a leader?" I asked.

"Well, lots of people follow her style of dress and
like to mimic her," Beth answered slowly. "That makes
her a leader, right?"

"I'd have a problem calling her a leader," I admitted, "even though she is well known. You see, I can't
advise anyone to live the way Madonna does. Living
the way she does is more likely to lead teens into trouble than to a happy life." Then I pointed out some of
the problems I could see ahead for anyone who followed the ideas the singer portrayed:

Her song "Material Girl" could make you think that
  all that matters in life is money.

Sexuality is the focus of her message. You can see it
  in her music and her life. She dresses in erotic
  clothing—on and off stage.

When she's in the news, it isn't for her thought-
    provoking ideas. It's for what sells sex!

"Is that the kind of leader you would advise your
younger sister to follow?" I asked Beth. "Would you
want to follow her yourself, if it meant her lifestyle
would impact your happiness for years to come?

"Take a closer look at what living this way would
mean. Would you like to be just like her? What will
happen if you follow the character and morals
described in her song? What if you became a 'material girl'—just out for money—or only had relationships
that ended in sexual encounters?"

It didn't take Beth long to figure out she'd probably
find herself in deep trouble in a short time.

Charles Barkley, the Phoenix Suns basketball player
says, "I'm not a role model; I'm a basketball player."
He has a clear picture of the difference between leading
and being in the newspapers, and I think it's good he
does. His physical prowess on the court helps him lead
his team to victory, but young people should watch
out before they decide to follow his lifestyle. He may be
famous, but I think it's good that he doesn't hold himself up for others to follow.

Fame is impressive, but it isn't leadership, because
leaders are people of whom we can say, "I want to be
just like him," or "I'd be proud to have the character
qualities that everyone can see in her life." How many
famous people can you honestly say that about?

Just because someone is popular, you can't assume
he or she will be a good role model. You won't want
to build your life on everything all famous people do
or say.

Separating Fame from Leadership

Let's also look at the flip side. Does being a leader mean you will become famous? If you become a leader, will you make the news and have newscasters clamoring to interview you?

Not necessarily. Real leaders may never live a glamorous lifestyle; the "good life" may escape them.

Why? Because fame and fortune are not what real leadership is all about. Leadership is about character—being able to look at yourself in the mirror and feel proud of the things you see. It's about taking a stand for what you know is right, even if it won't make you popular.

If you have doubts about the truth of that, ask yourself about two famous leaders—Martin Luther King Jr. and Abraham Lincoln.

Did they have an easy life?

Were they always famous and popular?

Did they have to fight for what they believed in?

What was the final price they paid?

Neither of these leaders had an easy time of it. When he made his now-famous speech in Washington, Dr. King had not attracted much fame and popularity. He suffered a lot for his stand. Only today can we admire him easily—from the distance time has brought.

President Lincoln fought to end slavery—earning himself many enemies along the way. Even when he was in the White House, many made fun of him and his policies.

Ultimately, both men died by assassins' bullets.

Sure, some people may earn fleeting fame for things that did not require the kind of sacrifice Lincoln and

King made. But will anyone remember what they've done a hundred years from now, as we remember Lincoln? Will they have changed the course of history, like King? And if they are remembered, will they be in the same class as these two men?

It's not likely.

The Cost of Leading

Why would anyone want to be a leader? I asked myself when I started writing this book. After all, it takes about five times as much integrity as sitting back and going with the flow. It takes enthusiasm and character. And they don't come easily.

Leadership that counts isn't a cakewalk. For anything that lasts, you'll pay a price. So let's start counting the cost.

Sacrifice

The number-one word that describes what it takes to lead is servanthood. People who lead—really lead—put themselves out for others, even when it's uncomfortable. They put themselves on the line for the good of others. They will sacrifice when they need to.

Most people don't find that glamorous and exciting. They'd rather have a fancy home than see that someone in need has housing. They'd rather get on the evening news than serve the people who elected them by protecting and fighting for them in Congress.

How many of our leaders would still serve if it meant they would never get the fame?

Time

Effective leadership will cost you a lot of hours. You'll have to put forth effort, even though it does not feel comfortable, and you may want to spend your time elsewhere. Anything less will not create the kind of leadership that changes lives. For example, if I have to write another book or prepare a speech, I must spend a lot of time in a quiet place, grinding out the words and ideas. That means I can't spend as much time with others—and I *like* to spend time with people!

Once I've prepared the speech, I get to do the fun part. As I'm standing in front of hundreds of people, about to share my ideas, I start to feel the enthusiasm. Adrenaline flows through my body, and it feels exciting. Finally I get to see some of the results of my work

Fame is impressive, but it isn't leadership.

when people tell me how my words changed their lives, caused them to think, or challenged them.

But I wouldn't have much to say, and I wouldn't influence many people if I never spent the lonely time writing it out.

I love to speak about the miracles God has done in my life. Yet I don't often talk about the hard work and investment of time that staying close to him requires. Being spiritually strong means I have to sacrifice, too.

Many days, when I turn to God, part of me would rather be playing a game of tennis, watching TV, calling a friend, playing cards, or doing a host of other things. But doing those things will not build a spiritual discipline that keeps me close to my Creator. To love him and learn from him, I have to block out a time, early in the day, when I can pray, write in my journal, and memorize Scripture.

Following my feelings would be easy—but it would never make me a leader. I would much rather invest my time for eternal rewards.

Delayed Gratification

When you take a stand as a leader and make important decisions, you won't always receive instant gratification. If you do, be on your guard—because it may not last long. Often, things get more difficult after a hard decision is made. You may feel all alone and wonder if you did the right thing.

Jim was willing to put off popularity and comfort for a larger cause. He wanted to start a Bible study in his high school, but this was several years ago before student-led Bible studies in high schools were approved by our constitution. He really took heat for his desire to help other Christians grow in God's Word.

For the first several months, only three people met with him on Wednesday mornings. Other students made fun of him and called him names when he walked down the school halls. It didn't stop him. He felt God had called him to be a light in the dark of his liberal high school. He was ready with a lesson each and every Wednesday morning. Everyone thought he would give up but he didn't. He kept putting his notices for the study on the bulletin boards even after others tore them down.

His conviction and enthusiasm were contagious. People admired his determination and loving attitude toward those who tried to ruin his dream. By the end of the year, thirty kids were meeting weekly with him. When he brought special speakers in, as many as sixty to seventy students would show up. Because Jim took the risk and stuck by his decision even when it was difficult, he was finally able to see the rewards of his work.

Hardship

Hardship will not deter leaders. When others fall in tough times, the leaders keep on.

Have you ever thought about what it took for Jesus to lead his disciples? The twelve men lived with him for three years. They prayed and played with him. When he showed his awesome power over nature, they watched: They saw him calm the sea, heal many people, and raise people from death. But they didn't believe—even after all that time and effort.

Jesus had a hard time with his thickheaded disciples, but he never gave up.

Neither can you, if you want to be a leader. Will you hang in there when:

People don't praise you for doing something difficult?
You do the right thing and aren't even noticed?
The newspapers never print your news?
No one lights up Broadway with your name?
People get angry with you for taking a stand?

Worth the Cost

If you decide to lead others, you will pay the price in sacrifice, time, delayed gratification, and hardship. Some days you'll struggle to find your way or get the energy you need.

"What's the use then?" you may ask. "I could never be that perfect. I may as well give up today."

To be a leader, do you think you must:

Never get tired?
Never feel as if you weren't worthwhile?
Never differ from the crowd?

If so, you've set your expectations too high or misunderstood my message. Everyone poops out, makes mistakes, and has regrets. You can't become the kind of person I'm talking about on your own. You'll need to stay in close touch with your Creator, who knows your frailties and can help you overcome them. God knows how weak we are, that we all sin and want to be on center stage. But he has also challenged each of us to be someone special. When we become leaders who follow him, we touch other lives and make him proud.

You can be that kind of person.

Leadership Do's

You'll have to do three things to become a leader.

1. Start right where you are. How well you are known won't necessarily be a reflection of your leadership skills, but who you are and what you do has a lot of impact on whether or not you become a leader. So don't wait to become famous before you start to lead.

Frequently (but not always) people who lead well become known for the quality of their lives. Even when the papers never pick up on the stories of people who feed the homeless or seek to bring reconciliation to warring parties, for example, their touch on the lives of people around them can have a powerful impact.

Leadership starts with your own willingness to become the kind of person others can admire and respect. You do that by filling your life with good character qualities and wise decisions.

2. Have something you believe in and be willing to stand up for it. Leaders have a goal worth reaching for—one that may not include popularity, gaining everyone's

People who lead—really lead—put themselves out for others, even when it's uncomfortable.

agreement, or getting elected class president. What are you willing to take heat about and not give up? Identify those things that are worth the pain.

At a recent book convention, I saw a man running around and talking to reporters, with his hair awry and one shirttail hanging out. He looked a mess. While everyone else was beautifully groomed in order to appeal to the bookstore people, this man's appearance stood out in the crowd.

Who was he? Randall Terry of Operation Rescue, someone who can stand out in any crowd. Many people disapprove when his group blocks abortion clinics. For some he's a bit too brash. I admire him for fighting for a cause he believes in. His personal appearance and notoriety pale beside the cause God has placed on his heart. His is a magnificent obsession—a cause that will make the world a better place. He's willing to fight for it, and I admire that.

What cause or purpose can you get that excited about?

3. Pay the price. Leading others means you have to pay a price. For example, you may lose friends and have to give up watching your favorite TV show because you've given time in your schedule to helping someone with a problem. Perhaps you'll stand out because you suffer for what you believe in. But the real way to leadership is fighting for what you know is right, following your heart, living out the dreams God placed inside you, and settling for nothing less.

CHECKPOINTS ✔

1. What misconceptions have you had about leadership? List them below. Do you have a hard time giving them up?

   _____

   _____

   _____

2. How did you develop your ideas of leadership?
   Name a few things that have influenced how
   you think about this subject.

   _____

   _____

   _____

3. What people have you looked up to as leaders?
   Name three people you admire from history,
   today's world scene, or your personal life. Why
   do you admire those people? Do they fit the def-
   inition of leadership that we've considered here?

   _____

   _____

   _____

4. How do you stack up against these leadership
   qualities? What might keep you from becoming a leader?

   _____

   _____

   _____

Who Leads
the Leader?

I came here to learn how to lead other people," a woman stated shortly after the start of one of my leadership conferences. "But all you've talked about is me! When do we get to the real leadership stuff?"

Her question wasn't unusual. People often wonder at the way I begin leadership sessions. That's because they have certain expectations about such training: They figure leading begins with other people. When they enter a session, they want to know how to make others follow their lead, how to win over an important client, and so on. So it's a shock when they find out that the starting place for leadership can't be others. We start by dealing with the person who wants to lead.

"Strong leaders must control themselves, first," I explained to this woman. "People who can't take care of their lives don't have what it takes to influence others. Before you affect the lives of others, you have to look at what kind of person you need to be."

That's where I start with anyone who expresses interest in leading. And it's why we will spend the next chapters looking at your own life. You need a clear idea of who you are and what you have to offer before you try to tell others what to do.

Teens Who Want to Lead

Many people come to me and ask my advice on how they can become leaders in their schools, homes, and communities. Whether the question comes from a teen or adult, the place I start is always with the would-be leader. I get to know teens who ask my advice by talking to them about their lives and what they want to accomplish. In a few minutes, I try to discover something about each person. That little bit of information can influence what I say.

After John heard me speak a few times and looked over my books, he decided to follow in my footsteps and become a public speaker. So he called me for advice, then wrote me a three-page letter.

From our brief contact, I could see that John had some skills that could help him reach others. He also seemed sincere in his desire to reach the goal he'd set. But I didn't suggest that he start developing as a speaker, and I didn't encourage him to contact others who could show him how to lead.

John had not proved to me—or others—that he knew how to lead his own life. He had recently abused alcohol and drugs, causing pain and suffering in his life and to people around him. A short jail term had even been involved. Now, less than a year later, he wanted to guide teens.

The ideas you accept about yourself will drive your opinion of your abilities and will affect your goals.

I'm not saying John can never become a leader. He may someday inspire thousands. But he needs to prove himself first. He needs to show people he can stay away from drugs and alcohol. He needs to practice the ideas he wants to talk about by putting them to work in his own life.

Otherwise, why should anyone believe that he can hold out when times get tough? How will people know that the moment he faces a challenge he will not turn again to drugs? I advised John to start his leadership by taking control of himself. He needs to increase his credibility before his message will have much impact.

Do you need to gain control of something in your life before you can speak to others? Perhaps your stumbling block is not as serious as a drug problem, but you can still have an out-of-control place in your life that needs attention.

Like John, you may not be ready to lead today, because you have a spot in your life where growth is needed. That deficit could interfere with your ability to lead well. Work on that spot, and turn yourself into better leadership material.

Susan, a student from the Midwest, didn't want to speak publicly, but she did want to help others. When she talked to me about starting to counsel others in her school, I noticed that she had good advice that could help her friends and others. The deep pain in her past helped her pick out the hurting people around her.

But I didn't counsel Susan, either, on ways she could reach out to others. I could see that she still felt very angry about the people who had hurt her, and her emotions would have hindered her message.

"Don't try to lead yet," I advised her. "There are some big areas you need to grow in first. Get your act together now, and in a little while you may become a terrific leader." I suggested that she spend time learning to get along better with her parents and to deal with some problems in her home. Once she's established a good track record, I hope she will lend a hand to others.

"I guess wanting to help others was really a cop-out for me," Susan admitted near the end of our talk.

I asked what she meant.

"You see, deep in my heart I knew that I needed to face my parents—and maybe even find some counseling. But I wanted to help someone else so I could take my mind off my own pain."

I felt proud of Susan because she quickly realized that leaders need to lead themselves first. She was ready to do what it would take to make herself into a leader.

If, like Susan, you have identified problems in your own life, don't become discouraged and give up reading this book. In these pages you can learn how to take the steps that will turn you into a leader. You'll discover actions that can build leadership in your life because we're going to spend a lot of time on the subjects that will help you most.

What You See Is What You Get

To lead people well, you need to know—and like—yourself. Otherwise, that negative attitude will show through all your efforts, and you won't do a very good job of leading.

Loving and accepting yourself isn't always easy. Each year hundreds of young people write me, saying they don't like themselves. Though they may not use these words, the focus of their questions is, "What could I do in this world? How can I make it a better place when I have no hope for myself?"

Many of them are like Kim, who wrote me saying:

Dear Bill:
   I hate life. I have nothing to live for.
   My parents and I barely get along—you could say we just exist. We communicate by yelling and scream-

ing at one another. Though they tell me they love me, I don't believe it. They are never here.

You wouldn't believe the pressures that have been put on me in high school. This is my last year, and I am ready to explode. Nothing is happening the way I wanted it to.

Some people say I will regret seeing high school end, that I will miss the fun and friends. I don't know what they mean, because my life isn't fun at all. These are some of the most painful days I've ever lived through. Everyone else seems so perfect because they put on false faces. When I try to match up to them, I fail.

I need your help. You said you would write us individually. Please write me back.

I don't know how much time I've got, so write fast.

Hurting,
Kim

That message comes through loud and clear in many of the letters I get. Each teen has been caught in a trap and feels as if there is no way out. These teens feel alone in the world, never suspecting that many people they know are going through the same thing.

Their predicament can be expressed in a five-part formula that goes like this:

1	+	2	+	3	+	4	=	5
Our perception of ourselves		Leads to how we feel about ourselves		This results in what we do (our actions)		Actions become the habits		That form our lives

It can be summarized this way:

Perception + Feelings + Actions + Habits = Life

That equation illustrates that you can't change the sum (your life) without changing the other parts of the equation. You'll need to start with the first part of the formula—how you see yourself.

People in prisons frequently consider themselves losers. Many were raised by parents who told them, "You'll never do anything good with your life," so they didn't. Today they see themselves as the unfortunate people, the bad ones, or people to whom nothing good ever happens. They may blame their problems on fate or luck because they don't understand that certain actions in their lives resulted in positive or negative results.

Contrast those people with Danny. He walks down the hall at school with his eyes wide open and a smile on his face. He looks everyone in the eye, and when he talks to someone, his focus doesn't stray. You won't get the feeling that he's waiting for someone more important to come into the room. When you talk to him, you feel like a million dollars.

Danny has a healthy opinion of himself. He likes himself for what he is and sees himself as a good, worthwhile person. He's got a pretty good handle on the perception part of the equation.

If you aren't like Danny, don't be jealous and decide to give up. You, too, can develop a healthy perception of yourself. That's what we are going to cover in the next few chapters. Here you can learn more about yourself and what you can be.

See Yourself as You Are

When it comes to your opinion of yourself, what you believe is what you get, because your actions will reflect your thinking. So you'll need to deal with the thoughts that have gotten you where you are today.

Do you regularly remind yourself that you are special and have capabilities you can use for good? Or are you so busy finding fault with yourself that you feel unfit to give someone a hand with an after-school chore, help your sister with her homework, or take part in a church function? Continually focusing on your negatives will lead you to a dead end.

If you have a lot of trouble believing in yourself today, don't let things stay that way. There is help out there. My book, *Stand Tall,* was written to help teens learn to like themselves. If the person you see in the mirror makes you unhappy, *Stand Tall* will help you discover practical ways to improve your perception of yourself. You'll learn about teens who struggled with their self-images and won, improving their views of themselves and their outlook on life.

When I met Jake, plenty of things seemed to be going wrong in his life. His opinion of himself was pretty low.

"Do you want to change?" I asked him. "Because you can, you know! See yourself through God's eyes and the eyes of your parents and people who believe in you and are pulling for you." I asked him if anyone had ever encouraged him.

"Yeah, my math teacher, Ms. Brown, used to tell me I had a lot to offer the world."

"Well?" I waited expectantly.

"Well, I couldn't listen to her, could I? After all, what does she know? The kids I hang out with know me better than she does."

"Instead of believing in the good points someone sees, you've been accepting the opinions of a few teens who always put you down," I pointed out. "They get their kicks by destroying your self-worth—but you are the one who chooses to listen to them.

"Start focusing on the people who believe in you," I advised Jake. "Listen to them and start accepting what they say as truth. In a while, you will see a big change in your life."

What was true for Jake is true for you, too. The ideas you accept about yourself will drive your opinion of your abilities and will affect your goals. When you hang around with people who can't see the positive side of your life, you doom yourself to living in the negative, and accept a lie that keeps you from becoming your best.

Fight back against such lies by finding out who you truly are. You can do that when you focus on the positive in your life—your gifts and abilities—and put your efforts and emotions into those things.

Personal Evaluation

Begin now to change your focus, and concentrate on the things that make you feel good about yourself. Take a good look at yourself by asking the following questions. As you answer, focus on your positive points or identify practical goals for change. Decide now—before you start answering—not to turn this into a pity party, but use it to set some constructive goals.

1. What are my strong points? (Name some character qualities, some abilities you have developed, and so on.)
2. What are some areas I need to improve in? (Where do you need to gain strength of character, gain skill in an ability, or learn more, for example?)

Tough Leadership

One of the reasons you need to like yourself as a person before you lead is that leadership will bring many personal challenges. Every leader needs dedication to keep going when leading becomes tough. Practice the following four steps in your life, because they will form a basis for your other leadership skills.

Meet High Standards

If you want to be a successful leader, you will need to set high standards for yourself. That's because real leaders never expect others to do what they would not do themselves—in fact, others will usually do a lot less than the people who lead them.

Suppose you wanted to coach football. How would you start? Why, you'd have to become a player first. When you had spent your time on the field, stood up to the attacks of other players, and felt the pain, you would have earned the right to show others how to play the game. No player would respect you if you simply walked on the field, saying, "I'm the coach," and had never sweated through the practices, learned teamwork, and made the sacrifices that are part of playing well. If you didn't even know the plays, how could you tell others what to do?

Hang Tough

Enjoyment isn't the most important thing to a leader. When the hard jobs come, a leader will make the effort to learn the skill, spend the time working out

Leaders who settle for second best cannot help others become their best.

a goal, and do what has to be done. Discipline enables real leaders to reach their goals.

Every summer, when I go to a fair and enter the 4-H barn, I see young people who have learned discipline. Every day they feed their animals, clean their pens, and take care of their needs. All those hours of mundane chores lead to the moment in the limelight, when they are handed the ribbons that say they've achieved their goal. But no one watching the awards sees the times these youngsters got up early in the morning to feed their charges or stayed up late with a sick animal.

Leadership isn't always getting the glory—you'll have to face some pain, first.

Face It Alone

Greatness is often built on time spent alone. In order to create his master works, Johann Sebastian Bach spent many hours alone at his organ. Without that time of solitude, he could never have shared his greatness with the world. Michelangelo spent many hours conceptualizing his paintings and sculptures. He spent huge chunks of time with only a paintbrush or chisel for company. When people enter the Sistine Chapel today, they admire his work. But how many people who look at those pictures remember the hours he spent on a scaffold, apart from others?

Never Settle for Second Best

Leaders constantly look for new ways to do old things, for better ways that have never been tried. Don't settle for less than your best—whatever that is. Put forth the effort it takes, and you will eventually see the results.

Leaders who settle for second best cannot help others become their best.

The Greatness of You

You don't have to be another Bach or Michelangelo to be great. Greatness is everywhere, and though God created millions of things in this universe, there will never be another you! You have the potential, ability, and personality you need. Find out what God has for you by learning discipline and developing a godly character.

In these pages, we'll consider the kinds of character and skills that can make that happen. You'll learn ways to stand out from the crowd by making a difference.

CHECKPOINTS ✔

1. Why is it so important to know how to lead yourself before you lead others?

_____

_____

_____

2. This chapter described some teens who were not ready to lead. Why weren't they ready? What goals did they need to set before they led others?

_____

_____

_____

3. Are you happy with the way you are today? Write a letter describing how you see yourself. Explain why you feel good about yourself or why you think you need to improve.

_____

_____

_____

4. Describe your perceptions, feelings, actions, and habits. What kind of life has so far resulted from those factors? Do you need to make changes?

_____

_____

_____

5. If this chapter was difficult for you and you need some help seeing yourself clearly, talk to an adult you admire and are close to, such as a parent, teacher, or pastor. Ask that person to help you identify your strong and weak points. See yourself from another person's point of view for a while.

_____

_____

_____

Inside Stuff

Sure, I have a pretty good family life," Jeff stated. "And I guess I'm not the best guy around, but I'm not the worst, either. But doesn't being in charge take a lot more than that?"

He's right. Leadership takes something else, too—inside stuff. Being the kind of leader who will honor God takes all the character you've got (and some you haven't yet developed). Leaders need a few special character qualities based on those we considered in the last chapter.

I've identified three things teens will need to develop within themselves before they try to change the world.

Self-Knowledge

What kind of person are you inside? Do you know who you are? Can you identify some of your weak areas? Until you can answer those questions, you can't step in front of others to show them the way. That's because your vision for leadership rests upon what you know about yourself.

How has God blessed you? Are you good in some areas? Do you have important strengths you can bring to your leadership style?

When he was on the court, Michael Jordan knew he had special talents and abilities—while he was playing professional basketball—that he used to his fullest. Becoming a world-class player took a lot of effort, but he put it out. He also knew when it was time to quit, however: when he was being unfair to his team because he could not offer the kind of concentration his job required. He knew himself well enough to know it was time to stop—at least for a while.

Self Test

Learn more about yourself by taking stock of what you are and what others think of you.

1. What do you see as your greatest strengths and weaknesses?
2. What would your family describe as your strengths? Weaknesses? Ask them for their input. Be willing to work on areas they identify as less than perfect.
3. Write down your greatest fears and joys.
4. In what areas has God really blessed you?
5. What life's work or purpose do you feel called by God to perform?

6. Who do you admire most? Why?
7. If you had to describe yourself with a Bible verse or story, which one would it be?
8. If you had ten minutes left to live and were in a room with a total stranger, what would you tell that person?

I hope these questions helped you understand more about yourself by showing you what means the most to you. Did you find certain ideas coming up over and over again? Perhaps they identify things that you focus on the most.

Self-Control

How do you react when you come face-to-face with something pleasurable that you also know is wrong? Can you control your eating, talking, and thinking? Do you do your homework first—or put it off till the last minute because it's not fun? Do you fret and get discouraged when you face troubles? When you do what is right, even though it is difficult, you are showing self-control.

Getting control of your actions is an important investment of time if you are looking to lead. When you spend time pursuing long-term goals, you show what's really important to you. When you turn away from doing what seems like "fun" because you want to invest in your future; when you get into God's Word because you want to be close to him; or you answer yes to the Holy Spirit when he calls, others will know you can turn aside from selfish desires and give them your best. They will be willing to trust you and follow your lead.

Today you may not see the point of turning aside anger when it threatens to overwhelm you or saying no to a date who wants to spend the night with you. "Will it really matter ten years from now?" you may wonder.

It will! Learning to say no to temptation builds your self-control in small ways that could pay dividends for the rest of your life. Develop the abilities God has given you today and look forward to the time when he places bigger responsibilities in your hands. Building self-control will launch your future on an upward swing instead of a downward slide. You will not have to feel the pain of being used—because you said no to dates who wanted you to share your body and "go all the way" before marriage. You won't abuse your children when they cry because you've learned to control feelings of anger and frustration. You won't be like the teen who went along with what a friend wanted—and killed a person. Now he's spending time in prison because he lacked the self-control to say no.

People don't admire others who have no self-control. I saw a poll recently that identified the most and least admired athletes. Mary Lou Retton was most admired; Mike Tyson was the least. No one looks up to a man who cannot control his actions.

Humility

Most people don't associate the word *humility* with leadership. They picture leaders as people who sit at head tables, ride in big cars, and bark orders into phones.

But wise leaders understand the servant attitude that makes a great leader. They recognize that a leader doesn't do all the talking—he develops listening skills.

Instead of grabbing the front seat, a leader will often sit in the back. She will not treat her brothers and sisters like dirt, even if they do get on her nerves.

Instead of looking to improve their own situation, Christian leaders must seek to be the servant of all—because that is what Jesus did. He gave up his glory in heaven to be despised and ridiculed on earth. He was unjustly accused and beaten; he had a crown of thorns thrust on his head, and a spear pierced his side. Though God's Son did nothing wrong, he suffered a cruel death

Learn more about yourself by taking stock of what you are and what others think of you.

on the cross and even descended into hell, so that we would never have to suffer the torments of hell ourselves. Yet in all that, Jesus displayed the humility of true leadership; author Bill Hybels called it "descending into greatness."

Humility doesn't mean you must become a doormat; it means you become loving, considerate, and kind. With the Lord in your heart, you can let others do most of the talking, get most of the glory, and win most of the prizes. You can appreciate the successes of your friends without getting jealous or do a good deed without getting the credit.

We have taught our children the Bible verse that says, "But many that are first shall be last; and the last shall be first" (Matt. 19:30 KJV). We've told them that it means that if you have to be the first here on earth, always getting the recognition, you will be the last in God's sight. But if you are willing to be last on earth and let others go first (even in the food line), God will be pleased with you.

Recently I visited my sister and received a lesson in servanthood. At bedtime, my sister and her husband made up their bed for my wife and me. Though we offered to sleep in the living room, they didn't take us up on the offer. "We want to learn to be more humble and Christlike," they told us. They want to learn to lead the way Jesus asks them to.

I know how difficult it can be to learn humility. All my life, I have wanted to be on center stage. The applause that comes with all that attention feels good, and I've learned to seek it. Recently God has been showing me what humility is all about. The lesson hasn't come easily to me. I've had several friends love me enough to confront me with the fact that I talk too much about *my* accomplishments, *my* dreams, *my* goals. They said they have felt second best. I've even noticed that it's hard for me to enter into a conversation about other people's interests if they aren't the same as my own. I've been challenged by God to realize that *I* need *him*—he doesn't need me.

Save yourself the kind of painful lessons I've had to learn and put your energy into something better than applause and recognition by learning to be humble. Learning to be a humble leader will prepare you to help others and effect changes in their lives. Being part of something so positive can bring you much happiness.

On the other hand, if you seek to lead only to be the top dog, to hear the applause and win the awards, you may succeed; you may become first in everyone's eyes. But you will never be first in God's eyes. You'll never experience true leadership.

The choice is yours: to settle for the approval of men or develop the inside stuff that will make you the leader God wants you to be. It's up to you.

You Have What It Takes

Sometimes ordinary people have the best leadership skills—even the ones who don't like to give a speech in front of the class or don't usually gain all the glory on the team.

That's because leading isn't just about doing all the fun things—saving a friend from sad consequences, getting a name at school, or being recognized as one of the best counselors in your class. It's about doing the things you need to do, taking a stand when you need to, and keeping your life in good shape. Lots of teens can do those things—even the shy ones.

"But my life is so boring," Danny complained as if that would disqualify him from leadership.

"Lots of leaders have lives that aren't that glamorous," I pointed out. "In fact, being a leader may make your life seem dull to others. I've seen leaders whose lives seem boring because their day-to-day tasks are not exciting. Maybe they don't hit all the parties—but they do the things that make them leaders, things that need doing. They reach out to others in ways that the 'party animals' never could."

What kind of qualities was I talking about? Simple ones that every teen can handle. Are you the kind of leader who:

- Gets enough rest to stay strong physically and emotionally?
- Would rather miss a few parties than neglect a few responsibilities?
- Eats right?
- Keeps the promises you make?
- Exercises regularly?

If you have not developed those habits, you've missed out on a lot of leadership opportunities. You've limited yourself to a go-with-the-flow lifestyle. But even if you lack *all* those qualities, don't despair—make the above list into a set of new goals. Carry the list in your wallet or purse and review it regularly until your goals become new habits.

Walk Your Talk

If you want to be a successful leader, you'll need to walk your talk. People will have to see your commitment to a positive lifestyle. You can show your leadership abilities to the world:

By living in harmony with your family, because you learn people skills in your home.

By leaving your room clean before you leave for the mall or the shore.

> By becoming a peacemaker with your brother or sister before you try to advise your friends.
>
> By staying away from alcohol and drugs.
>
> By focusing on others, instead of only yourself.

You must walk your talk every day, in the things you do and what you say. Your conduct reveals much about your attitudes and character.

Andy was not walking his talk when he came to me. He complained, "I've done what you said and tried to be a leader, but it never seems to work. My teammates never give me any respect. When I went out for captain of the team, I didn't make it. I guess Mr. Davis had it in for me—'cause my friends and some other people said I should have had the spot." I could practically see the chip on that football player's shoulder; no one in the class could have missed his unhappiness with his situation.

Andy was so busy focusing on himself and what was wrong that he missed the biggest part of the reason he never got respect: He had not yet learned how to give it. Instead of finding ways to become a better team member, he berated the teens around him. He never tried to make another player look good or help a class member. And he complained about the coach.

When he learns to walk his talk and develop the inside stuff first, people may begin to notice him. Jesus said it best: "It is the thought-life that pollutes" (Mark 7:20). It is what comes *out* of a man that defiles him because those actions reveal the inside stuff that may be polluted.

It's the same for you. Concentrate on building inner strengths, and you will find the development of other—

more obvious—leadership skills much easier. You may not find crowds wanting to follow in your footsteps as you spend time on the unglamorous things; but many will want to be near you all the same. People who listen well usually attract people who need to talk. Good friends make more new friends. A person who smiles is a pleasure to be around. So when you develop inner qualities, they will begin to show on the outside as well.

Costly Leadership

Getting attention for your leadership qualities won't be all gravy, though. It will challenge you to live up to high standards when the going gets tough. For example, you can preach to people about loving their parents, but they probably won't listen until they see how you love your own mom and dad. So you'll have to show your friends the way—even when your dad doesn't come to the game or your mom needs your help on the day you'd planned to go on a picnic.

If you want to lead, you won't only do what comes easily. You may find it hard to look others in the eye as you pass them in the hallway at school. You may feel awkward trying to leave politely when others tell dirty jokes. But if you're intent on being a leader, you'll find yourself doing these types of things more often.

"Hey, I'm just not that perfect," Bert complained. "Aren't you expecting an awful lot out of me? Seems like that's a tall order!"

His complaint would be right on the money—if I expected you to be perfect and to do it all on your own. I'm not saying you'll never face a problem or that you'll never make a mistake. But I have faith that you can become a real leader—if you are willing to put

God first in your life, that is. He's the one who will enable you to stand up to the trials and win out. With him at your side, you can turn away from whatever is wrong.

> But remember this—the wrong desires that come into your life aren't anything new and different. Many others have faced exactly the same problems before you. And no temptation is irresistible. You can trust God to keep the temptation from becoming so strong that you can't stand up against it, for he has promised this and will do what he says. He will show you how to escape temptation's power so that you can bear up patiently against it.
>
> 1 Corinthians 10:13

This verse means you can always say no. God always gives you a way out, another answer or alternative, when you have a big problem that's about to overwhelm you. If you have trusted in Jesus as your Savior, no temptation will be too hard for you to handle.

It is possible, I suppose, that I might offer my children ice cream, show it to them, and then pull it away. But God never plays tricks like that on his children. He will not allow you to be tempted beyond the point where you can say no. Even if you've struggled—and failed—to stop smoking, you can start running your own life today by taking on that challenge—and winning!

When teens say they can't stop smoking, I ask, "Could you stop for one minute?"

"Certainly."

"How about three?"

"Of course!"

"How about four," I suggest, "if your life depended on it?"

"I guess."

"How about five—if your kids' lives depended on it?"

"Okay, maybe."

"What about six, if the whole universe would fall into the deepest lake if you didn't?"

By now I hope you see what I mean. If teens who wanted to quit took their battle a minute at a time, they could stop. They do have the ability to do it—as long as it's broken into small steps.

Concentrate on building inner strengths, and you will find the development of other—more obvious—leadership skills much easier.

Bert still wasn't convinced. "You know, I still don't think I could do it. Leadership—that just isn't me. I'm just a loser—ask my family."

"Don't fool yourself," I advised him. "Maybe you have faced tough times before this. But even though you feel like a loser, you can still become a chooser. God made you, and you are special. Let him show you how to make decisions, and you'll become more than you can imagine today."

Even though I don't know your background or upbringing, your strengths or weaknesses, I can still say that to you.

Do you know why?

Because God does not make mistakes. He specializes on the inside stuff, like knowing right from wrong, having honesty, integrity, and loyalty. Each of us has those tools to do the job; all it takes is putting forth effort and doing it God's way.

Sure, if you want to wallow in your sin, chances are almost certain you will never lead anyone anywhere— except maybe into your own condition. But if you believe in something greater than yourself and start to work on the person you see in the mirror, you will go places.

I've seen it happen countless times.

CHECKPOINTS ✔

1. What weak areas in your life would interfere with your efforts to become a strong leader? Why would they do that? Do you have a plan

to overcome them? If not, develop one with a
friend or adult who is close to you.

_____

_____

_____

2. Do you have self-control? Humility? List some
   ways you have shown them lately. How have
   you blown it recently? What has helped you
   back on track when you have blown it before?
   What has not worked for you?

_____

_____

_____

3. What qualities do ordinary people have that
   make good leaders? Are they part of your life?
   Can you build them into your life? How?

_____

_____

_____

4. What bad habit do you need to overcome? Can
   you do it for a short time? What keeps you from
   getting it under control? Develop a plan to get
   yourself back on track. If you need to, talk to a
   friend who will check up on you once in a while,
   to see if you are overcoming the problem.

_____

_____

_____

Don't Just Be a Leader

reat leaders do not only lead—they also know who (and when) to follow. If you want to lead, you'll need to find someone worth following—someone who will show you how to become the kind of leader you can be proud of.

Perhaps you've wondered where you can get the inspiration, encouragement, and respect for yourself that you will need to become a real leader. This seems awful tough, you may be thinking. I don't think I know anybody who can do all that.

It will have to be a special kind of person.

The Ultimate Leader

When you seek someone to follow, I would counsel you to settle for nothing less than the best. Learn from the ultimate leader of all time.

This man never made a salary that could compare to Michael Jordan's. He never appeared on a Barbara Walters special. Nor did he write a book that appeared on the *New York Times* best-seller list (though his book is the best-seller of all time). He never owned his own house, car, or tennis shoes. He died penniless, even losing his clothes to the people who killed him.

I hope you have realized that the leader I am talking about is Jesus Christ. Though he lacked a lot in physical possessions, Jesus knew how to stand and fight for a cause. He did it in the temple, when he took on the "religious" people who used God's house as a place to rake in money by stealing from others. Jesus called the spot a den of thieves, knocked over their money tables, and confronted their greed and hypocrisy.

But the same man was gentle and humble, too. Jesus didn't lead by insisting on his rights. He gave up his divine position and "humbled himself and became obedient unto death, even the death of the cross." God called him to lay down his life, and he obeyed. He became the ultimate servant of mankind.

But, you may protest, who wants to be that kind of leader? Bo-ring! I'm looking for some fun and excitement. I'm no monk or nun. I'll party till I puke; now that I'm old enough to drink, I deserve it.

While you are heading down that path, realize that your attempt to satisfy yourself and impress others will make you a slave to your desires and fears. Your greatest need will be to fulfill your earthly pleasures. You'll step on board the roller coaster named "Pleasure-Seeking Nightmare."

Every time someone else has a nicer outfit than yours, you will want it. Even a closet full of clothes will never be enough. All your fashions, cars, houses, and toys will own you. You will never honestly be able to claim you own them, because getting and keeping things will control your life.

No clothes, method of transportation, or home controlled Jesus. No one, not even Satan, could buy him with the pride of life, the lust of the eyes, or the lust of the flesh.

> Then Jesus was led out into the wilderness by the Holy Spirit, to be tempted there by Satan. For forty days and forty nights he ate nothing and became very hungry. Then Satan tempted him to get food by changing stones into loaves of bread.
>
> "It will prove you are the Son of God," he said.
>
> But Jesus told him, "No! For the Scriptures tell us that bread won't feed men's souls: obedience to every word of God is what we need."
>
> Then Satan took him to Jerusalem to the roof of the Temple. "Jump off," he said, "and prove you are the Son of God; for the Scriptures declare, 'God will send his angels to keep you from harm' . . . they will prevent you from smashing on the rocks below."
>
> Jesus retorted, "It also says not to put the Lord your God to a foolish test!"
>
> Next Satan took him to the peak of a very high mountain, and showed him the nations of the world and all their glory. "I'll give it all to you," he said, "if you will only kneel and worship me."
>
> "Get out of here, Satan," Jesus told him. "The Scriptures say, 'Worship only the Lord God. Obey only him.'"

Then Satan went away, and angels came and cared for Jesus.

> Matthew 4:1–11

Not only was Jesus able to withstand temptation, he was humble enough to love little children, even when it meant putting off the important people. Though adults were pressing for his time and attention, Jesus did not push the youngsters aside with an excuse.

But Jesus said, "Let the little children come to me, and don't prevent them. For of such is the Kingdom of Heaven." And he put his hands on their heads and blessed them before he left.

> Matthew 19:14–15

He even compared the kingdom of heaven to children, because each of us must become like a helpless, trusting child before we can enter eternity. We need to understand our great need and be willing to depend on someone greater than ourselves. God wants us to need him the same way a child needs a parent.

Unlike superstar athletes who charge their fans for autographs, Jesus didn't seek money or adulation. Instead of looking for attention from others, he served them. Just before he gave up his life, Jesus washed his disciples' feet and left them with this command:

And since I, the Lord and Teacher, have washed your feet, you ought to wash each other's feet. I have given you an example to follow: do as I have done to you.

> John 13:14–15

Follow the Leader

Just because Jesus was a servant-leader, however, doesn't mean you can treat him as if he were your maid. Don't expect him to do everything for you and jump at the snap of your fingers. Instead, become the kind of servant Jesus was. Wash the feet of people at home, in school, or at church.

Wash Feet

How do you do that? You simply help others. Do for them what you would do for Jesus—or the most famous person you can think of—if he were with you right now. Don't do it to get noticed, but secretly help your mom, your little brother, or your neighbor.

When a neighbor is hungry, don't just wish him well; provide him with a loaf of bread. Don't stop at praying for someone who needs to know Jesus; invite her to church, too, so she can hear his Word.

God will reward you for your servant spirit—not by making you Miss America or giving you a red sports car—but with happiness and satisfaction that will make those things seem cheap and unimportant.

Plug into Power

You'll want to become as much like Jesus as you can—in every way imaginable. For example, you will want to take advantage of the wisdom Jesus showed when he was burned out or around people for a long time. If you're leading others, realize that you still need time alone. At the height of Jesus' ministry, when everything was going great, he spent time praying to his Father and meditating on God's Word and purpose for his life. No matter how glorious his miracles and message were, he still needed to get alone with his Father.

So spend time alone with your heavenly Father. Plug into his power. Get your strength from him spiritually, and you will be refueled to lead others better.

Forgive and Encourage

When you or others around you goof up, do you know how to handle it? Jesus was the ultimate leader when it came to dealing with mistakes—even when he saw those mistakes coming from a mile away.

The Gospels show how Jesus acted when Peter goofed up in a big way. The night he was betrayed, Jesus told Peter, "Before the cock crows at dawn, you will deny me three times!" (Matt. 26:34). He said the words firmly but lovingly.

Peter did fail Jesus that night, but he also realized that the man he had betrayed was the ultimate leader; because he knew Jesus was who he claimed to be and was worth following, Peter turned around and began to follow him again. God restored him before too long and even gave the apostle more courage and conviction than ever. After the resurrection, Jesus encouraged the man who had denied him to become a leader who would stand out for the cause of his gospel.

Jesus did not simply feel sorry for the fallen Peter. He had empathy for his follower—he felt for Peter deeply, knew what he was going through, and provided an answer. Jesus got in the middle of his disciple's problem, cried with him, and went through the trouble at his side.

The same great leader would like to be there for you. He would love to be your friend, Lord, and Savior—someone you can trust with all your problems. He came to earth wanting to do that for you.

But you, in turn, have to be willing to believe.

When Jesus stood before Herod and Pilate, these leaders in the Roman Empire expected to see miracles or hear excuses. But Jesus had already spoken the words the Father had given him, and he kept silent. For three years he had done the miracles, and now it was time to give his life. Nothing but the testimony he had already given was offered.

Today he may not do miracles on a street corner, but Jesus offers you the same testimony.

I challenge you to put the ultimate leader in charge of your life. Ask him into your heart, so you will hate evil, and possess the power to be victorious over sin. Meet him face-to-face and heart-to-heart. He wants you to open your life to him.

If you do that, Jesus will be your strength when you hurt. He will heal your pain and comfort you when you worry. Jesus is the only one who can change your life and give you all the strength you need. With that, you will become a stand-out leader.

Stand-Out Leadership

Many teens have stand-out leaders in their parents— Mom and Dad are great communicators, and their children are following in their footsteps.

But what if your parents were failures in the parenting department? Do you still have a chance? Of course! You can change by looking for other examples to learn from. Just look for the people who know how to stand out, and follow them!

My friend Rick Newton is a stand-out leader who has carried a cross around the world for the last seventeen years and has walked thirty thousand miles with it.

Rick and I went to Russia together. We arrived in August 1991, three days after the attempted coup. We had come to distribute Bibles and landed in the middle of a political incident.

Well, our interpreter didn't show up—and neither did our Bibles (which had been shipped separately). For two days, we didn't even have a room.

But God was not stymied. We constantly asked each other, "What is God going to do now?"

No matter how glorious his miracles and message were, Jesus still needed to get alone with his Father.

For starters, he had already miraculously provided Bibles. Before we left America, James Robison, an evangelist from Texas, met Rick in the airport and offered us five hundred children's Bibles—written in Russian. Though the two men seemed to bump into each other by "coincidence," I didn't believe it was coincidence at all. God, who holds stars in the sky and makes our bodies work so amazingly, can make two men meet in an airport.

On the first day we gave out those children's Bibles we had brought with us, but we needed an interpreter.

That evening, in Red Square, Rick led a young man to the Lord. God provided our interpreter in the person of that new Christian.

For ten days, that man took an almost-two-hour subway ride to be with us for twelve hours, so we could speak to people. He wanted to share his newfound hope in Jesus Christ. Hundreds of people heard the message he spoke for us.

One evening we got home late and I went to the hotel store to get some colas. A small girl from America came up behind me and asked, "Mister, would you please help me? Our refrigerator doesn't work, and I can't explain it to this lady, because she doesn't understand English."

I used sign language to communicate with that woman.

Back in the room, Rick again asked me, "What is God going to do?" We didn't have any more Bibles because the ones we had paid for still hadn't arrived. I told him how I had met the little girl.

Ten minutes later, the little girl knocked at our door. Her father wanted to thank me, she said.

"God's ready to work. I can feel it!" Rick commented as I went down the hall. Rick was right! The girl's father, Bob Weiner, just "happened" to work with Christian Youth International. When he heard we wanted to distribute Bibles at Moscow University, he offered us fifteen hundred of the fifteen thousand Bibles he had on hand.

If you don't let God lead you, how will you have the courage and conviction to stand for him? Whether you go into medicine, politics, law, music, or sports, you will be just a follower until you commit yourself to someone who can help you stand out and lead.

Start looking for ways in which God can lead you today. Learn to ask yourself, "What is God going to do now?" If you want to lead, don't worry about what people will say or do. When I go into schools and hand out my pamphlets that talk about my faith in God, when I share from stage how God has been faithful and restored my marriage and given me hope and peace beyond understanding, people ask me how I do it.

"Aren't you afraid you won't get booked for any more speeches?" they want to know.

I tell them that God has protected me in many times and different places. He will continue to do so.

Be like David who told people that God had saved him when he had faced wild lions and would protect him from Goliath as well. Follow the Lord continually. Obey your parents and the law because doing those things will make you a good follower who can someday become a good leader.

Learn to ask yourself, "What is God going to do now?"

CHECKPOINTS ✔

1. When you think about the fact that Jesus had so few possessions, how does it make you feel? Why?

   _____

   _____

   _____

2. Do you own your possessions, or do they own you? How do you know? Do you think you need to make changes in this area?

   _____

   _____

   _____

3. List four attributes of Jesus that made him a great leader. Why do you think these things were important? How can you improve your leadership by following his lead?

   _____

   _____

   _____

   _____

4. Have you ever tried to treat God as if he were your maid? What happened? How can you avoid having that attitude?

   _____

   _____

   _____

5. Did this chapter challenge you to know Jesus? If so, have you asked him into your heart? Here is a simple prayer you can use: "Dear Jesus, I have made many mistakes and sinned before you and others. Please forgive me and take over my life. I'm sorry for my sins and I want to live for you. Please help me. Please be my Lord, Savior, and Best Friend. Thank you very much." If you are already a Christian, how did this chapter affect you? Pray about the things you have learned and ask God how he wants to use them in your life.

_____

_____

_____

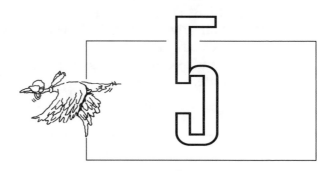

The Other Side
of Leadership

We've spent a lot of time looking at you—who you are and the qualities that will make you a good leader. But there is more to leadership than you. No one can lead without considering the part others play. You'll need to know how to get along with others and how to evaluate the impact they have on your life.

Because others influence us every day—and we influence them in return—in the next chapters we'll take a look at the other side of leadership: the people around you.

See Others as They Are

If you want to lead, you must learn to see people accurately. Everyone has good points and bad points, but sometimes we only see one side of a person. And sometimes we make the mistake of measuring ourselves by others—what they do or what they think of us.

Such comparisons can kill your self-esteem in a moment. In fact, it's the number-one cause of inferiority. It can kill even the best vision you have for yourself.

How does that work? Easy. When you see another teen who looks perfect, do you ask if she has problems—just like you? She may appear to have it all now, but do you consider that she may be making choices that could cost her tomorrow? Probably not. Someone else's life may seem perfect in comparison to your own, but are you seeing the whole picture?

Nearly everyone in my high school admired Chuck and looked up to him. All Chuck had to do was change his hairstyle, and the male half of the school followed along. He was a great athlete, and he had lots of friends and plenty of dates. Everything seemed to be going great for him, and I sure envied him.

While Chuck partied, though, he became addicted to alcohol—and ended up an alcoholic. He had to marry his first wife while he was still in high school, and that responsibility killed his plans for a professional sports career.

Today none of my old high school friends know what happened to Chuck; and I'm not sure how many times he's been married. No one from the old crowd admires Chuck's life today.

We all looked on the outside and thought Chuck had it made, but we were wrong. That's because we couldn't see the whole picture. We should have been looking for some inside qualities like:

- Honesty
- Integrity
- Self-discipline
- A willingness to serve others
- An ability to help others become successful
- Pride in the school
- Love for others (not just dates)
- Respect for parents
- A sense of community responsibility

Those things were missing from Chuck's life. We did not see him as he really was because our vision had become clouded by his popularity.

Sometimes you will ignore a popular person's faults or limitations. At other times you may ignore a person's good points because you don't like his "package," the way he looks. Either can cause you not to see what is really there.

Can You See What Others Could Be or Do?

When you look at others, do you have the ability to envision the potential for greatness in them? To find out, answer these questions:

- Can I see goodness in my family, friends, and acquaintances?
- Can I recognize greatness in my friends?
- Can I acknowledge others' abilities and suggest how they can use them?
- Can I envision worthwhile goals that will help others tap their potential?

Did you answer yes to all four questions? If so, you already have a vision for leading others. Do your best to build on that.

If you only answered yes to three, identify where you need to build your leadership skills. Right now make out a plan that can help you. Your plan might look like this:

Step 1: Pick a few friends and observe them.

Step 2: Notice a positive quality they possess.

Step 3: Tell them that you notice this quality and encourage them to use it more in school, sports, social occasions, or at home.

Step 4: Ask your friends what you can do to help them reach their goals.

You will be on your way to habitually bringing the best out in others. Leaders make other people feel good and look good. Go and give it a try!

If you only said yes to one or two, make a conscious decision to think of others and learn to encourage them. Look at some people who could become your role models. Learn from them how to lead.

Encouragement Exercise

If you need to build your ability to recognize greatness in others, start in your family. Can you appreciate the talents God gave your brothers and sisters? Maybe your older brother is good in sports, your sister is talented in writing, and your younger brother is handy with mechanical things. What can you do to help them achieve in these areas? Start to help them and encourage them to do their best with their particular talent.

Now practice sizing up other people in the same way. When you practice seeing the best in others, you'll increase your vision for them.

Every person has been given skills to develop and use to benefit others. Help your friends discover what gifts God has given them and encourage them to use those abilities to achieve their goals. Challenge your friends to fulfill their best dreams.

Look through the eyes of others, feel through their hearts, and help make this world more than it was when you came into it. Perhaps you will challenge your friends to stand out and do their best. On days when they have trouble seeing their goals, renew their vision. Help them to keep hoping, and you will pass on to them a point of view that most people lack.

Giving Up or Holding On

When is it time to give up on people? I met a principal whose answer to that was "never." One of his teachers became exasperated with a student who always made trouble in her class. But the principal recognized that the troublemaker was acting in a loud, disruptive way, always bringing attention to himself, because of the pain in his home. This boy was a full-time discipline problem, which made both teacher and class miserable.

One day the teacher went to the principal and asked him to remove the boy from her class.

"I can remove him, if you don't mind giving up on him," he answered.

"I don't want to give up on him. I just want him out so I can have a better class," she explained.

"We can get him out of there. If you think we should give up on him, then we will kick him out immediately."

Someone else's life may seem perfect in comparison to your own, but are you seeing the whole picture?

"It's not that I want to give up on him. I just can't teach with him there!" exclaimed the frustrated teacher.

"The moment you want to give up on him, let me know, and I will have him put someplace else."

Finally she understood and replied, "I will never give up on him."

Most of us would like to have someone who will never give up on us, who will always keep holding on. And we do. God has given us many more chances than we deserve, and when we fail, he waits patiently for us to run into his open arms and grab the strength, hope, and determination he has to offer.

Pass on that hope. Is there a friend or classmate you've been tempted to give up on? What can you do today to offer a little strength, hope, and determination to that person?

You may even be able to find ways to encourage people you don't even know personally. Mr. Fitzwilliam, a farmer in North Dakota, had a vision for youth. Though he had a gigantic farm to tend to, he worked hard to bring in Christian speakers who could present the truth to the kids in his area. He spends some of his spare time now as chairman of a group that schedules speakers on a regular basis. He does not know every teen at the rallies he arranges, but he is making a difference in their lives.

Not everyone needs encouragement, though. Sometimes you'll need to challenge or confront the people who you have a vision of greatness for.

A couple years ago I visited on a TV show called *Action Sixties,* with Herman and Sharron Bailey. After the show, we went on to Herman's radio station, where I talked about one of my books.

A listener called up to give me "what for" about what I had written. This non-Christian enjoyed giving Christians a lot of trouble. She argued with everything I said.

Finally I lost my cool, for the first time, on the air. "Honey, don't you have a job?" I asked. "Is calling up and causing trouble all you have to do? Wouldn't it be better for you to get a job and work for an employer? Are we holding you up, honey?"

All the time we talked—about twenty minutes—Herman had a smile on his face. Though he could see me dying on the air, he let it go.

But when he drove me to the airport, Herman taught me something I will never forget. "Never attack a person personally," he advised me. "Stick to the issues—attack the issues. If you are against abortion, and the person is for it, stick with why you believe abortion is murder. The moment you called her 'honey' and attacked her, you lost all your credibility." He talked to me for forty minutes, and I wrote down every point he made.

A few days later I used that information when I appeared on a television show in which the hostess attacked me personally. I stuck to the issues and turned it into a wonderful interview that did me a lot of good. I'm grateful to Herman Bailey for being willing to lovingly confront me and show me how I could improve.

Look for Ways to Bring Out the Best in Others

Can you be the catalyst that makes someone see things in a fresh way? Can you challenge those about you to brainstorm ideas and come up with possibilities that could help solve a problem, improve someone's life, or reach people for God?

Perhaps today you will encourage a faltering student to keep on studying—and someday she will discover the cure for cancer. Maybe you will challenge your brother to reach out to the world and end hunger or discrimination—and he will change society. Your vision for loving and complimenting could help someone become so much more.

Tips for Complimenting Others

1. *Be sincere.* Don't say it if it's only flattery.
2. *Use their name.* People love to hear their names spoken.
3. *Make eye contact.* Don't look elsewhere when complimenting someone. It suggests you have something to hide.
4. *Be specific.* Say "I like the way you respect your mom." Not "I like the way you get along with people." It's too vague.
5. *Be brief.* Compliments shouldn't go on and on. You'll only make the other person uncomfortable.

Rich Mullins, the Christian music artist, went back to school so he could get his degree and teach at-risk kids on an Indian reservation. He also took two days out of

Challenge your friends to fulfill their best dreams.

his busy schedule to talk and sing and offer encouragement to a fan he'd never met before. I was that fan. His compassion is affecting the lives of others. You, too, can encourage creativity and touch the lives of others.

Tips for Helping Others Be More Creative

1. *Encourage others to dream.* Ask "What if . . . ?" What if you could do anything for a living? What would it be?
2. *Build others up.* Everyone does better when others help us feel good about ourselves. Be an encourager.
3. *No wrong ideas allowed.* Creativity is like brainstorming. If you think it, say it. Be positive. Be daring.
4. *Make a list of creative ideas.* Write them down—this makes them personal and adds power to them.

5. *Create a plan to make one of these ideas a reality.* Get help from someone who is a positive-thinking, strong-willed, risk taker. They will give you the encouragement you need. Go for it!

CHECKPOINTS ✔

1. Do you often compare yourself to others negatively? Describe how that feels and why you do it. Are you seeing others clearly when you do it? How are you seeing yourself?

   _____

   _____

   _____

   _____

2. How do you see other people? Can you encourage them toward their goals? Can you help them learn what they can become? Can you challenge them to do better tomorrow than they have done today? Think of someone you have encouraged recently. What did you do? How did it influence that person?

   _____

   _____

   _____

   _____

3. Have you practiced giving someone a sincere compliment? If not, review the steps and make someone's day.

_____

_____

_____

4. What can you do to be more creative yourself? Who did you help develop their creative powers? Take a risk, step out of your comfort zone, and make the world a better place.

_____

_____

_____

5. How do right and wrong influence your goals? Review your goals carefully. Do you need to reevaluate any of your planning to avoid doing wrong?

_____

_____

_____

Leadership Close to Home

F amilies are the places we learn to lead—or follow. For some teens they also present one of the toughest leadership challenges. So let's take a look at the influence family life has on your ability to lead. We'll also consider some things you can do to improve things, if your family doesn't always make things easy.

See the Good in Your Family

When you learn to look intelligently and accurately at others (something I mentioned in the last chapter), you can begin to apply that kind of clear vision to your own family. Maybe you've only seen the bad side of Mom and Dad in the past—you've focused on the times they wouldn't let you go somewhere or made a mistake that hurt you badly.

Do you see your parents as they really are? Do you realize that they have troubles, too? Unless you understand that, you are sure to be disappointed when they let you down or make a poor decision.

Unless your parents abuse you, they are probably trying to do a good job raising you. They may not be perfect, but they want to help you become your best.

Teens who are abused—verbally, emotionally, physically, or sexually—need to realize that their parents desperately need help. Deep-rooted pain has taken over their lives, and it needs to be pulled out.

Many abused teens write me and ask me to keep their secret. Since I have to help those teens and their families, I try to make them see their parents accurately—as hurting people who need help to break the cycle of abuse. No teen should have to go on suffering from Mom or Dad's problem or anger. Help is available! Here are some suggestions for teens who find themselves in abusive situations.

1. Speak up. Tell someone you trust about the pain you are suffering or seeing at home. Many children save their fear-stricken mothers from years of physical abuse by refusing to be silent any longer. Get it out in the open.

2. Remember, it's not your fault. Parental problems such as abuse, alcoholism, anger, or divorce aren't your fault. You are the victim. You don't deserve to live like this.

3. Talk to a counselor. It's vital that you get your feelings, fears, and frustrations out from inside you. Go to your school counselor, aunt, older brother, friend—

anyone you trust can help. A professional Christian counselor or your pastor may be the most helpful.

4. Take courage. You are breaking the cycle of pain by getting help. Your action can decrease your family pain. You are very brave and wise when you stand out for your family's sake. Get a trusted friend to stand by you. God is with you; the pain *can* stop.

Parent Evaluation

Like anyone else, your parents have strong and weak points. This evaluation will help you understand more about them.

Remember as you write to be fair to your parents. If you have trouble seeing one side of your mom or dad's character, what gets in your way?

1. What are your dad's good points?

    _____

    _____

2. What are some areas in which your dad needs to improve?

    _____

    _____

3. What are your mom's good points?

    _____

    _____

4. In what areas do you think she needs to improve?

    _____

    _____

When you evaluated your parents, I hope it did not become an attack or an opportunity to simply pat them on the back. Instead, I hope you could look fairly at your home life. If you have trouble doing that, perhaps you need to talk to an adult who can help you get a balanced picture.

Does your family have a team spirit? Can you give up things for one another, because you all have a higher goal? That's what you are shooting for, if you want to be a leader.

Why? Because leaders need to have role models that live out the right things in their lives. They don't need to spend years building up anger and resentment. They don't need to head into adulthood missing the skills that will help them love others. They do not need to develop bad habits that will stunt their lives for many

Talk to your mom and dad and let them know you want something more—a real family team!

years. Leaders need to extract positive skills and abilities from their family lives.

As I spoke at an evening seminar once, I noticed several families with teenage sons or daughters sitting with them. They laughed and enjoyed life and were obviously proud of one another.

Afterwards, as is my habit, I asked some of these successful parents why they seemed to enjoy their teenage son's company so much, or why Dad felt comfortable enough to drape his arm over his daughter's shoulders. The answers all reflected a feeling that they all felt part of something bigger than themselves. The family is the first and most important place for creating an environment in which people feel needed.

Alissa and James's parents told me they did not create chores for their teens—they gave them responsibilities. If Alissa did not do the dishes, they didn't get done. That meant the house did not function. She and her brother got the message: We need you to do this. Not only did they do the day-to-day things, James and Alissa got to help decide where the family went on vacation, how they would go, and so on. They read the map and made some calls for reservations. In this home, all four people were important parts of the family.

Other teens who come to my seminars sit in the corner of the back row, alone. Their arms are folded and their heads held low.

I also try to speak to these teens. Many of them have no meaningful connection to their families. They have never felt needed and appreciated, and now they feel like losers. Their situations break my heart.

Building Family Skills

If your parents have not made you feel needed at home, they may not have learned the skills that would enable them to do that. So do what you can to help them change that. If you need to seek counseling together, encourage them to join you.

I grew up in a very dysfunctional family that taught few of the life lessons I needed. A few years ago I had to face the fact that I needed help to learn to love myself the way I was. You see, for years I had tried to cope with the pain from my family background by being a success—the family savior who would do things no one in our family had done.

So I ran my own business from the time I was seventeen, wrote nine books, and traveled around the world in an effort to feel good about myself. But until I received Christian counseling, something was still missing.

I want to make sure my kids don't have the kind of home I had. Instead, I want to have fun times with them, to teach them the meaning of forgiveness, and help them have a healthy life.

If you need help, seek it out.

Let your family know you need to be part of something greater than yourself. Do it while you have time at home, because once you grow up, you may never take the chance. Learning to be part of the team, the job, the organization, is something you need to practice today. At home you get the chance to argue and make peace—so practice your leadership skills by making peace before you go out into the world.

I encourage parents to learn how to become coaches. In the fall, the high school football coach may become the most influential person in town. Why? Because he makes each team member feel truly needed. He can get teens who never study to hit the books; he has junk-food junkies eating right, and the most rebellious teens following all his rules. It's all because he's taught his team the importance of acting like a team—working together, acting responsibly, helping each other.

I try to teach parents those skills, but sometimes it has to start with a challenge from their teens to create this kind of life. So talk to your mom and dad and let them know you want something more—a real family team!

Families Can Help

Families can love you and support you in a special way. They can tell you things you might never hear from a friend. I know, because I have a brother, Dale, who has been courageous enough to do that for me.

I will never forget the day my brother loved me enough to challenge me, face-to-face, about my pride. Though many people had thought about it, no one felt comfortable about approaching me.

Dale had come to my house, and we were sharing coffee and talking about the weather, kids, sports—surface chatter. That's when my brother told me he wanted to say something that was important to both of us.

"Do you realize that you are more impressed with yourself than with anyone in the world—including God?" He let me have it between the eyes when he spoke those words, and I didn't take it well.

"What are you talking about?" I demanded.

He pointed out that I have an overbearing, dominant personality, especially when I'm bragging about one of my speeches or my latest book. "You talk about your books, your speeches, all the kids you've led to the Lord recently, all the wonderful things you are doing, your itinerary, and so on.

"You expect others to get excited about you, but people are tired of hearing about *you* all the time. From time to time, you have to notice *them.*

"I've also noticed that you don't give God the credit the way you used to," he added. "You are wonderful

just as you are, Bill. But don't talk only about yourself,"
Dale said. He challenged me to focus on other people.
"You'll have a lot more friends that way, and life will be
better for everyone."

We ended with angry words and stopped just short
of a fist fight.

As my brother drove away, disgusted with me, I
slammed the door. *How dare he say that about me?* I
wondered. *I have helped him many times!* My anger
boiled. I even thought of writing him a revengeful note,
to get even with him. But then God got ahold of me.
He spoke to my heart and said, "You can let this opportunity make you a better person or a bitter person."

If I had chosen to let my anger take control, I would
have ended up far from God. Instead, I followed the
Lord's leading to look up every Bible verse that had to
do with pride. I found out that God resists us, turns his
back on us, and does not bless us or hear our prayers if

**Don't let the
problems you
face today keep
you from a
better future.**

we become puffed up with pride or conceit. But he honors and blesses us if we develop humility.

Then I took a look at my own life. He showed me that my jealousy of someone else's success showed that I had pride. I remembered that I could not watch the TV show M*A*S*H because I felt jealous of Alan Alda's success. I'm not sure why I was jealous of him, I guess it's just because he reminded me of me. When I made a list of all the people I competed with or felt jealous of, I didn't feel very proud of myself. I knew I needed a lot of help.

Today pride still haunts me, but because I know it can ruin my walk with God, I work to control it day by day. Only the strength and power of the Holy Spirit can keep it in check.

As I struggled with my pride—and the selfishness that caused it—God led me to this verse: "So it is right for me to be a little proud of all Christ Jesus has done through me" (Rom. 15:17). When Paul wrote that, he was proud of God, not his own powers.

Are you as proud of what God is doing through others as you are of what he's doing through you? I asked myself. The answer was "no way!" I didn't want to give God the credit. Dale had been right about that. I felt wounded because my brother confronted my pride, so I lashed out at him.

I'm glad Dale lovingly challenged me to look at areas I need to work on. He wanted to see me become my best. Dale and I are closer now than ever. His courage and love for me made it all possible.

Maybe your family isn't very positive today. But you can help them change their perception of themselves—and their feelings. Then together you can change your actions, establishing ones that will make your lives happier. Soon such actions can become habits of a better life.

Don't let the problems you face today keep you from a better future. Take a look at who you are, where you are, and where you want to be. Plan ahead for your future, and it can improve drastically. Lead yourself into tomorrow, and you may find others at your side, asking how you did it.

CHECKPOINTS ✔

1. Is your vision of your family clear and fair? Are you building a leadership family? If not, what steps can you take to change your life?

_____

_____

_____

2. Did you do the Parent Evaluation? (If not, do it now.) What did you discover about your mom and dad? About yourself?

_____

_____

_____

3. Does your family have a team spirit? If not, why not? What steps can you take to develop one?

_____

_____

_____

4. How does your family rate on skills that make you feel loved and part of a group? Where do you see a need for improvement? How can you make a difference?

   _____

   _____

   _____

5. Has your family confronted you when you have done wrong or needed to improve? What happened? Did it make you bitter or better?

   _____

   _____

   _____

Needed: Special People

To be successful, a basketball coach needs at least five other people. An orchestra conductor needs dozens. A five-star general needs thousands.

None of these people can lead alone. And, of course, neither can you. A leader needs someone to lead. That's why real leaders are people who *like* other people. They like to be around people. They like to be a part of something bigger than themselves. Involvement in a group such as a Sunday school class, youth group, or church can make a person feel needed, and that makes them want to contribute even more. People who do not feel needed, wanted, or appreciated will not take part. It makes no difference if it's in the church, in a golf league, or in a profession, people who do not feel a part of something—something that involves people—will feel unfulfilled and will eventually quit. Then they seek a new job, church, or spouse, and it keeps going that way—for some people, it continues until the day they die.

People need to feel needed to really shine. That's why I want to challenge you to find activities that can help you become part of your community. Start with your neighborhood. Get to know your neighbors. If you have a neighborhood party, help out with the younger kids. Distribute flyers advertising the event.

Real leaders are people who *like* other people. They like to be around people. They like to be a part of some-thing bigger than themselves.

If you have an apple tree in your yard, share your fruit with your neighbors. We have several apple and plum trees on our property; when the fruit ripens, we share it with four or five neighbors, and they appreciate it.

When one of my books comes out, I sign one for each of my neighbors and take them around. Over the years, they have come to appreciate and understand my work. Because I share that part of my life with them, we have become closer.

Become needed and important in your school by joining certain groups. By doing that you will discover more about yourself and learn about your skills. When you join the ball team, you get to know your teammates better. As you sweat beside others, you become a team. Like men who have fought a war together, you may become lifelong buddies, because you have been there for one another. Even if your team loses, you will have gained by sharing a common experience.

Maybe you'd rather go out for basketball, band, student council, drama club, or yearbook staff. It doesn't matter. Become part of some team—the chess team, the cheerleading squad, or the pep club. When you do that you will enter a small group of people who have interests like yours. It will make you feel more like part of the whole school, simply by being active in a small part of it.

Small Group Support

Once you are part of a small group, you have someone to support you, encourage you, and redirect you when you miss the mark. That's the kind of Bible study I meet with each week. When someone hurts, we pray for him and help him; we call him on the phone during the week or stop by his office to see how he's doing. If a member is doing something he should not, we look him in the eye and tell him so. Then we support him through the problem.

Because we each know the others depend on us, we all do our lessons every week. No one wants to show up empty-handed. No one wants to slow the rest of the group down.

Belonging to the group gives each of us a feeling of importance. Because of it, we do a better job of living our Christian lives in public. We can hear one another saying, "Don't do this!" "You know better than that!" or, "You have the power to walk away from that temptation." Meeting with these friends has helped my faith grow by leaps and bounds.

Rich is a young man I know who, like many teens, has never felt part of his school. No one seemed to need him. He'd never been asked to join the student council, Future Farmers, yearbook staff, or any of the sports teams. He usually ate lunch alone, because he didn't have many friends. He never showed up at any of the games. Deep inside, he was hurting, but he never reached out to others or looked for help to overcome his fears. We all need other people. I'll bet there were other kids who would have loved to have Rich as a friend. And if he would have searched, I'm sure he could have found a group to belong to that enjoyed the same things he did.

As a leader, don't just become involved yourself; encourage others—especially those who don't feel needed—to join in activities. Make room for them in a small group, so they know someone cares.

As a leader, encourage people who are left out to develop talents you can see in them. Are you a sports star? Ask kids who are not on the team to ride with you to the game or hang out with you in the cafeteria. Are you a member of the yearbook staff? Ask someone to help you cut and paste some afternoon and introduce him to the rest of the staff. Are you involved in the school play? Enlist someone to help you with your lines, and treat them to a shake afterward.

Leaders who do this really save lives, because they help people begin to feel needed. A few acts of kindness can change one teen's life.

About ten years ago, I challenged nineteen hundred high school students to pick up their trays and sit with someone who didn't have a friend. We all know those people; they stand out because they eat alone and usually are not attractive.

A few weeks later, I got back a letter:

Dear Bill:

I knew who you were talking about. Everyone makes fun of her. I never have personally, but I never stopped it, either. As you said, I was just as guilty and as much to blame.

But I finally picked up my tray, though it took me a week to get up the courage. I started to walk over to be her friend, and you are right, people do follow leaders—a couple of my friends came with me.

All four of us laughed and cried. We apologized for not coming sooner, because we had met a new friend. We had the greatest meal ever and will never forget it.

We met a girl just like us, with ambitions and fears.

I'm glad I took you up on your challenge, because that girl died two days later. The whole school found out that for the previous two years she'd had a disease no one knew anything about. I guess that was why it was hard for her to make friends.

That letter also described the terminally ill teen:

She was shy; she never made eye contact, and she always had chalk on her shoulders. You see, because she was intimidated by other students, she walked right along the blackboard as she left class. She didn't wear fancy clothes, and being seen in public with her wouldn't help your popularity.

The teen who had written me smudged the last few sentences with her tears. I could barely read the words.

Perhaps the hurting teen you'll meet won't be terminally ill. She may be like Amy, a teen who doesn't really feel as if she is part of her family. No one asks for her input, and she feels alone and insignificant. As long as no one needs her, her leadership skills will remain dormant. But if the right leader steps into her life, who knows what might happen?

Feeling needed can really make your day. When my pastor calls me and asks me to preach at our church, I

The crowd may not follow you, but you will certainly not be ordinary—you'll be a leader.

get all excited. Why? Because I feel needed. When a neighbor asks to borrow a flashlight, I feel the same way.

All you need to do is go over to an Amy and include her. Let her know you need her today.

I challenge you to act on what you have read here. If you do, you can touch a hurting life and truly stand out. The crowd may not follow you, but you will certainly not be ordinary—you'll be a leader.

CHECKPOINTS ✔

1. Are you part of something greater than yourself? Or are you just a passenger? Becoming part of a group can help your leadership skills grow tremendously. How can you make yourself part of the big picture?

   _____

   _____

   _____

2. What can you do in your neighborhood, in your school, and in your church to make you part of that group? Identify areas that people need help in and plan how you can take part.

   _____

   _____

   _____

3. Why are small groups so important? What benefits do they bring to people? How can they challenge people?

_____

_____

_____

4. Who are the people who have no friends in your school? Pick up your tray and sit with one of them. Make that person feel cared for and special. Write the name or description of one person you will reach out to this week.

_____

Following in Others' Footsteps

Whether or not we realize it, we all follow somebody. Maybe it's another teen who dresses in the latest styles or an adult who has accomplished something you aspire to. Or maybe someone else entirely. But the question is not, "Are you following someone?" It's "Who are you following?"

Who Do You Follow?

When you look around your school, your town, or your church, do you see people you admire? Do you follow them? Do you imitate people who have worthy goals? Or do you just follow a short-term friend down an easy path?

I'm not asking those questions idly. Many teens write to tell me about their poor leadership choices. Many teens live with the consequences of a poor decision every day—perhaps for the rest of their lives. Many have made a decision in the heat of the moment that they'd like to undo today.

"I thought Chuck was in love with me," Mary wrote me. "'He'd never do anything to harm me,' I thought. But that was before I found out I was pregnant. Just after I broke the news to him, he dumped me.

"I can't tell you how alone I feel at a time when I have to make a huge decision about the life growing inside me. I feel as if I've been used, and that's just what I think Chuck did to me."

Mary isn't the only person to be led astray by a guy. Girls often make poor decisions under the influence of a guy. And many guys start down the wrong path under a girl's influence. But it needn't be a member of the opposite sex. Bad influences come in every shape, size, and sex.

Recently I spoke to some gang members. Their leader promised that fame, power, and money would be theirs if they followed him. It was all a lie, as Micky discovered when he landed in jail because he followed the wrong leader.

Where Do You Follow?

Though most of us like to think we're pretty independent, the truth is we all have a deep need for someone to look up to. If we have a hard time finding a true leader, we may settle for one that isn't so good.

Such a man made the news a while ago. His name was David Koresh, and he led dozens of people to their deaths. People who were desperately seeking someone to tell them what to do, what to think, how to dress, how to act, and what to believe in gave their lives for a man who had led them astray.

But you don't have to follow a cult leader to be led down a wrong path. Sometimes you need only turn on the TV or pop in a compact disc. Subtle (and not-so-subtle) media messages capture the minds of people of all ages. In fact, I think they get away with pushing some of their bad ideas because we all have forgotten how to think, how to be the masters of our own destiny.

That easy trap of a go-with-the-flow mentality is why I encourage people to carefully choose who they will follow. It's simpler to allow leaders to make decisions for you—much easier than choosing your own plan of action—but it can be deadly.

Choosing a Leader

Before you follow someone, check him or her out. Boldness and confidence are not the only elements that make up a leader, so before you follow someone, know what he stands for. Look a little deeper than the outside—search for his values. That way you will know how he is likely to act and will be able to foresee the things that will motivate him.

Had the followers of David Koresh done that, they might have made a different decision. The cult leader promised that he was the Son of God and he claimed that the end was near. But his words were only cover-ups for selfish desires. In reality, this man never lived a godly life. The lies he told cost many lives. His path went the wrong way for a man who claimed to be God.

That's not the kind of leader I'm suggesting you should become—or the kind of person you need to follow. You must follow consistent, unselfish leaders, not those who will leave you feeling used and abused.

In Wichita, Kansas, I met the kind of leader teens can follow with confidence. Her name is Cheryl Hurley, and she is in charge of a ministry called High School Ministry Network.

Cheryl is a woman who has known the sting of pain. She went through a difficult divorce, and her daughter ran away.

God has given Cheryl the desire, love, and vision to reach out to teens. She wants to change lives for Christ, and to that end she took charge of eighteen Bible studies, all in different high schools.

Recently Cheryl brought me into one of the toughest high schools in Wichita. Prominent signs hopefully proclaimed, "Drug-Free School Zone" and "Gun-Free School Zone." Guards were posted at every entrance.

It took the students several minutes to settle down before I could be introduced. I had been told that even

The question is not, "Are you following someone?" It's "Who are you following?"

if I only spoke twenty minutes, they would appreciate whatever I could communicate to the teens. This was one tough school.

Well, I spoke for an hour and forty-five minutes, and a hundred teens stayed after to be counseled. During that time, these outwardly tough teens cried out their pains and learned to say no to going along with the crowd. I still receive letters from some of those students who are turning from the pressure to do drugs, have premarital sex, and drink alcohol and are learning to say yes to life.

From Cheryl I learned to have compassion and conviction. Prayer has kept her Bible studies going. She is challenging teens to stand up for their faith with a "See You at the Pole" event several times a year. As a result of Cheryl's ministry, many teens have learned not to be ashamed of Jesus.

Leadership Check

Before buying into any philosophies, you might want to check out a leader by asking yourself the following questions.

1. Is this a person of the Lord? Does this man or woman believe in Jesus and follow him every day? A person who will not live for God or who is noncommittal on the subject cannot lead you in God's direction. If she has no ultimate authority in her life, what will you be following? A leader who is more committed to himself than to the Lord could really lead you in the wrong direction.

Many people who have not discovered God as their leader turn freedom of thought into rebellion. Recently I met Anthony, who calls himself an atheist. One of the most important things in this man's life is education, and he has all the college degrees to prove it. But despite all the learning, he is empty inside, and you can see it in his eyes.

Because Anthony's life is empty, he tries to fill the space in many different ways. One week he tries booze; another week he tries to pick up women. He spends so much time at work that he's become a workaholic. But his compulsion to fill his life has only made him lonelier. His marriage is nearly ruined, and he has no close friends.

When I talked to Anthony, I learned that his father had never allowed him to talk back, argue, discuss, or share his opinion on any subject. He had to go along with whatever this unloving father decreed. That meant following a long list of things to do—and an even longer list of what not to do.

Then he shared that he had gotten very angry at a pastor who told him that some things were right and some were wrong and that people who did not choose Christ would burn forever. So Anthony turned against God.

His background helped me understand why this man always hated his bosses at every job. He'd had an earthly father who did not seem to love him, and he'd rejected the heavenly Father who could heal those hurts. I pray that some day Anthony comes to know his heavenly "Dad." But right now his life is one of rebellion.

Don't let yourself become an empty, lonely person like Anthony because you are unwilling to let God have first place in your life. Turning to him does not mean you add regulations to your life—instead you add life! Remember, a godly leader is one who knows and trusts God.

2. Does this leader put others first? Is he merely trying to please people, or is he considerate of others? That will not mean the person you admire should be a door-mat. He shouldn't starve himself while he feeds the world. But you should seek out a leader who takes pleasure in other people's accomplishments, and enjoys making others feel good.

The salesman who sells a million dollars of goods a year but never spends time with his family is not really a success. If a business owner grows his enterprise but treats his staff so badly that they all leave, he is also a failure.

Those who seek to be successful at the cost of others are not the kind of leader you'll want to follow. Find someone who puts others ahead of himself.

3. Does this leader get along with others? Relationship skills are part of any leader's abilities. Does he treat others with respect? Can she laugh at herself? When talking with others, is this person gentle or abusive? Notice if the leader you want to follow has good listening skills. Do others like her? Effective leaders get along with others.

Be careful, though. Be sure you weigh this skill with the first two qualities I mentioned. Many bad leaders seem to have the ability to get along with others. They may have a charisma that attracts others for a short time. But instead of motivating people, they manipulate them. Ask yourself, does this leader give his best to others—or take their best from them? Is she good at getting along with others—or getting what she wants out of them?

4. Is this leader humble or arrogant? Humility is one of the marks of a leader. A godly leader will not swagger or strut, but will say, like Paul, "If anyone is going to boast, let him boast about what the Lord has done and not about himself" (2 Cor. 10:17).

5. Does this leader try to please God or people? Whose approval is most important to him? Can she speak the truth boldly, telling what God has put on her heart? Look carefully at your life and the lives of those you follow. Make sure they do what God wants instead of finding ways to become popular.

6. Does he or she believe in strong morals and biblical values? Can he or she tell right from wrong? Real leaders believe in these things. You cannot convince me that a woman's right to have an abortion overrides a child's right to life. I have to stand up for that life. In fact, I believe the abortion question is the strongest issue of our day, and it will only be overcome by a leader with wisdom, courage, and tact. Believe in leaders who know what to stand for and how to do it. Watch and follow them, and you can become like them.

Never follow a leader who has trouble distinguishing right from wrong.

7. Can this person admit mistakes and faults and get help when it is needed? Quality leaders admit their mistakes instead of hiding them.

Many teachers who want to be leaders are kept from their best because they still carry their childhood pains. A teacher may have experienced a terrible childhood, or something bad may have happened to her, and she could carry that pain about, inflicting it on other people—including her students.

Real leaders learn to forgive and ask forgiveness. They can say, "I'm sorry."

Those powerful words have meant a lot in my life. I've noticed that my kids learn more about the truth, the Lord, and my life when I admit my mistakes.

A couple years ago I needed professional counseling to overcome the messages I received in the dysfunctional home in which I grew up. That willingness to get help saved my life—and has made me a much better leader.

8. Does this leader exhibit a forgiving spirit? A few years ago, a friend of mine lost her policeman-husband in a traffic accident, when he was working on an accident scene. A teenage boy who was watching the accident, not the road, hit and killed her husband.

My friends had their best years ahead of them. They had just begun to travel. Success had just found them.

At the funeral, several of this woman's children wanted to see the teen who had killed their dad. She would not permit them to meet the boy, but moments after the funeral, she had her son drive her to the boy's house. She walked in and introduced herself.

What she found was a devastated teenager and parents who felt his pain. She knew he would remember this tragedy and might carry it with him for the rest of his life. Because she didn't want that, my friend told the boy how her husband knew Jesus as his Lord and Savior. Therefore, she had every confidence he was in heaven. "God makes no mistakes," she told the teen. "We believe in a God who has a plan. Though we don't know why this happened, I don't want you to carry this pain with you for the rest of your life. So I fully and freely forgive you. Get on with your life," she advised. "Don't let this ruin you, because it was simply an accident."

That is radical love and forgiveness. That's the kind of example I could follow without hesitation. She was living out her faith in the world, and her light shone brightly. Pain would linger, and time would be the greatest medicine, but she gave that teen the chance to heal within.

9. Can this leader clean up his life before cleaning up the world? One of the first requirements the Bible lays down for leaders in the church is that they "must have a well-behaved family, with children who obey quickly and quietly" (1 Tim. 3:4). Why would the Bible say that? Because leadership starts at home. If a leader doesn't have control of his own life, you'd better not follow his advice for your life.

Choose your leaders carefully, instead of believing all that you hear. I want you to know the truth, and you can only do that if you take care in deciding who you should follow. Once you find those good leaders, hang around them enough and you will become like them.

Boldness and confidence are not the only elements that make up a leader, so before you follow someone, know what he stands for.

Then carry over the good qualities you learn to your own leadership. Use those skills when you lead and pass them on to those who you lead. Strive to be a number-one leader—one who follows Jesus Christ. When your leaders follow him, you can follow them. And then you can show others the same path that has changed your life.

Stand out for good!

Checkpoints ✔

1. Have you ever followed the wrong person? What happened? What did you learn from that experience?

   _____

   _____

   _____

2. Using the information on leadership you've read in this book, list some qualities that make bad leaders on the lines below. (Hint: What are some of the opposites of the qualities you know you should build into your life?) Are you following some people like this? What can you do about it?

   _____

   _____

   _____

3. Compare the attitudes of godly leaders to false leaders. Is there a big difference? What is it?

Godly leaders:

_____

_____

False leaders:

_____

_____

4. How many of the leadership qualities in this chapter can you see in yourself (even just a little)? How can you help them grow in your life? What kind of people do you need to follow so that this will happen?

_____

_____

_____

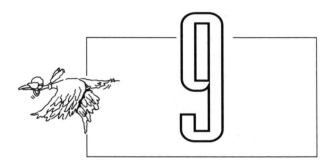

Leadership Homework

We've taken a careful look at you, your family, and the community around you. You've learned much about the inside stuff it takes to be a leader.

"Sure, I can clean my room," Pearl commented. "And I know how to study, even when I have to give up a party. Those are things you recommend that teens do. Yet I can't say I lead other people.

"Am I missing something?" she asked. "Maybe I need to spend time with someone who's famous, or hang around with someone who's taken a class in leadership—you know, have someone show me the ropes."

Leadership won't necessarily require all that from Pearl, but it will be demanding. It takes three basic things from anyone.

Good leaders live what they believe; they do what is right, even when they know they're going to take heat for it.

Desire: You have to want to change yourself. If you don't see the need to grow and feel the wish to change, you'll remain just what you are—a follower.

Know-how: That's what this book should give you. In its pages you'll find specific areas you can grow in and steps to take that will help you lead yourself and others.

Willingness to practice: The new ideas you learn about as you read this book won't stick until you make them part of your life. Whatever you don't use, you will lose. So plan to develop and grow in new ways—every day of your life.

If you've read this far, you must have some desire for leadership. By the time you finish reading, you will have plenty of know-how. Right now you need to start to practice the things that will make you a leader. Think of this as your leadership homework.

Put time into this homework, and you can develop leadership qualities that will make you stand out from the crowd. In the first eight chapters you've learned about the personal qualities you'll need. Now it's time to learn to put your knowledge into action.

Observation Assignment

Remember that, whether or not you realize it, you have leaders all around you whose lives can inspire you. Focus on some qualities you can see in these people. That will give you a close-up view of what you want to be.

Think of some leaders you admire. Perhaps they are:

- Your father, mother, or another family member
- A successful teacher
- A person on your block who brings people together
- Someone who helps the sick people in your community

Next make a list of the qualities you admire in each person. Identify how those qualities contribute to his or her success.

Leaders come in many shapes and sizes; they have different strong points. Perhaps your list includes some of the following keys I've found in successful leaders.

A Sense of Enthusiasm

Successful people usually get pumped up when they face a new challenge or begin a project. Once they are into it, they want to share it with others, so they express their positive feelings.

You may not be excited about everything—and I'm not suggesting you should be. Maybe you don't agree with all the plans your mom or dad has for your future. But I'll bet you have some plans that do excite you. When you think of what you'd like to accomplish in life, you get thrilled about making it happen. If so, you already have one important leadership quality.

Integrity

Good leaders live what they believe; they do what is right, even when they know they're going to take heat for it. They also avoid situations that could get them into trouble because they know it is not part of the lifestyle they want. Integrity is a way of life—in fact, that word is the best one I can think of to describe how Christians should live out their faith.

People like this are always aboveboard in their dealings with people. They wouldn't steal a penny and would return to the store if the cashier overpaid them. People like that qualify for leadership.

You may need to work on this area of your life. If you do, start today. Expecting no free ride, earning what you get, and treating other people honestly are a part of your leadership homework—so keep working at it.

A Willingness to Work Hard

Leaders put in a lot of hard work. They stick with projects to the end.

You've completed tough projects, too. Once you've gotten enthusiastic about the team, started to work with animals, or begun to learn math or music, you've held on. Make it your goal to finish what you begin, and to work as hard as you can—and then some.

A Willingness to Put Things on the Line for Right

Not everyone runs away from the pain that will bring gain and looks for the easy way out when doing right requires sacrifice. Some teens, like John, are willing to stand out from the crowd. One high-school senior wrote me:

Dear Bill:

I want to write you to let you know that everybody isn't doing it.

I had a great chance to be sexually involved with my girlfriend, but I turned her down, and I'm glad I did.

Neither one of us believed in premarital sex, but after about a year and a half, something changed, and she began pressuring me. All her friends were doing it, and she wanted to experience sex as well.

"We love each other," she said. "No one will know."

We had lots of opportunities to have sex, but I kept on saying no.

Last month I broke off our relationship. "I do not like having you need me so much. You are too dependent on me," I explained. "I also don't want to be in a position in which I might compromise on my beliefs and end up having sex with you." As much as I love her, I still know having sex before marriage is wrong. I would regret it—and probably wouldn't marry her.

This was one of the toughest things I have ever had to do, Bill, but you will never know how good I feel because of it.

Someday I know I will look back on this as one of the best things I have ever done for myself and her. If I ever meet her husband, I will be able to look him in the eye, knowing I did not take advantage of his wife.

Keep on with your message!

Still saying no,
John

John will feel the pain of losing his girlfriend. It may hurt him for a while, but he's put his future—and hers—ahead of some temporary pleasure.

When John wants to lead other teens who need to make tough decisions, his ability to choose what was right will help him feel for their hurt, but it will also enable him to encourage them to take the first, hard step. He will be able to use the example of his own life to point out the benefits of good choices.

Sometimes taking the stand for right means you have to put your friendship on the line. Recently I got a letter from Felicity, who was in danger in her home. Over and over again, she warned me not to tell anyone what she was sharing with me. She trusted me not to tell about the abuse she received.

Though I risked losing Felicity's trust, I had to make calls to get her help. If I had not acted, she might have experienced that pain for the rest of her life.

At first Felicity was angry at me. But eventually she wrote to thank me, and shared that I was the first person who cared enough to get her help. Now that her family is involved in counseling, she can see that I made the right choice.

If a friend tells you she is depressed and thinking about suicide, get her help. Go to her parents or another adult you can trust—a counselor, teacher, or principal. Don't promise to keep quiet. But even if you

---

Make it your goal to finish what you begin, and to work as hard as you can— and then some.

---

already promised not to tell anyone, you need to get help. You can apologize later for having made a hasty promise. But for now you need to stand out and help your friend, even if it costs your friendship.

Follow-up Assignment

Your leadership quality list may be very different from mine. That's because a lot of elements go into good leadership. There's a lot to learn about leading!

Other leadership skills you may already be working on in your life include:

- Sensitivity to people
- Ambition
- Communication skills
- Effort

- Appreciation for what others are and do
- Insight
- A desire to do God's will
- An ability to see the big picture
- The desire to grow beyond what you are now
- Excitement about improving yourself
- Caring for animals
- Concern for the environment
- Growth potential
- Frankness

You may look at these and think, I don't have many of those qualities. Before you consign yourself to failure, realize that everyone—even you—has some positive elements in his or her life. With work, you can develop these areas—and develop new leadership qualities to add to them.

CHECKPOINTS ✔

1. Do you have the desire, know-how, and willingness to practice leadership skills? If you feel that you fall short, what is holding you back? If you think you have everything you need, what is inspiring you?

   _____

   _____

   _____

2. Did you complete the Observation Assignment? (If not, do it now.) What kind of people did you choose? Were some of them obvious leaders, like teachers, pastors, and parents? Did you list some leaders who do not hold formal positions, yet knew how to encourage others?

_____

_____

_____

3. Can you think of leadership skills that were not mentioned in this chapter? List them below. Why do you think these qualities are important?

_____

_____

_____

Setting Your Sights on Leadership

We've looked at your need to lead yourself, the kind of follower you are, and the qualities you need to become a leader. But in order to become a real leader, you also need a plan, a vision that starts with yourself, and eventually extends to others.

Watch Where You're Going!

Have you ever bumped into someone on the street or in the school hallway and had that person say, "Watch where you're going!" It's not the nicest thing to say, but it's really very good advice.

As a leader, you need to watch where you're going. Develop a plan for your future. Design what your future is going to look like. Draw a map of how you're going to get there.

Start setting your sights on leadership by asking yourself:

Where do I want to go with my life?
What do I want to do?
What talents and abilities do I have that can help me?
What motivates me to do this?
What is my purpose in doing it?

Imagine what your life can be. Fantasize an exciting future for yourself—because if you can't think it, it will never happen.

You'll need to know yourself before you can reach out to others. Focus on the things you really want to achieve and put your effort into those areas.

Once you have developed this set of goals, you'll need to stick with them. Review them from time to time to keep them fresh in your mind.

A couple years ago I had a great opportunity to host a nationwide Christian radio program. Every Saturday night, for an hour, I would take calls from young people. We would talk about issues that were important to them.

I felt excited about a chance to challenge teens to stand out, become leaders for God, and stand tall as they walked through life. The national exposure looked good to me: More people could read my books, and my speaking engagements might expand as a result of this work. I wanted to do it!

Just at the right time, I met a wise man who asked me, "Does this opportunity fit in with your life purpose and the goals God has for you?"

"I'm concerned with reaching teenagers and helping them with their problems. But," I admitted, "I feel God has called me to the public schools, to reach the lost, more than he has called me to speak to those who already know the Lord."

"This radio station is a very conservative Christian station," my friend pointed out. "If you become famous at it, if it does work, you will become known as the Reverend Bill or some name similar to that. I think you should seriously consider this, because it might wipe out your ministry to public school kids."

I prayed about that opportunity and God made it very clear that I wasn't staying focused on his goal for me. The glamor of being nationally known had carried me away.

God did not want me to focus on this area, so I declined to do the show. Inside I felt a great peace.

Focus on the goals God has for you and keep striving for them, and you will begin to feel the same peace. Set your sights on what he has for you, and hold to that!

Map Your Future

Remember, we said that leaders need a vision. Part of your personal vision is your own future—what you can do with your life and how you can affect your world. Imagine what your life can be. Fantasize an exciting future for yourself—because if you can't think it, it will never happen. Tell yourself, I am going to make a great difference next year—and in five years. Now picture yourself doing that.

Draw a kind of road map—a personal treasure map—that depicts:

- What you will accomplish this month
- What you will achieve in six months
- What you will attain in a year
- Where you will arrive five years from now

Next, spend a few moments imagining those things coming true in your life, because that is the first step in making them happen. As you improve your thinking, you will begin to feel that you can do it. Then you will start making it part of your life.

It takes practice to change your thinking, but you may find it helps to put them on paper. I like to write down the things I plan to accomplish. That way my creative juices get set in motion. Many life goals that I have accomplished started with a picture in my head that I wrote out in detail.

Start actively imagining your own success, and you will begin to see changes. You'll be like MaryAnn, who wrote me:

Dear Bill:

I am so glad I read your book *[Stand Tall]*. A year ago I was listening to you in my high school gym, as you gave a talk. I didn't even want to hear you speak, but I'm glad I did.

You see, because of what you said, I realize that I'm not so bad after all. You have really helped me see myself as I am and as I can be.

I will never forget being eight years old and having my rage-filled father, who is an alcoholic, tell me I was a loser. Just before he left my mother, he turned and pointed to me, "You're nothing! You're a nobody! You will never amount to anything!" he screamed before turning away and walking out the door and out of our lives.

Since that time I've been through a lot of counseling, and with the help of many loving people I've begun to believe I truly am who God says I am. Now I can be what he wants me to be—someone who can make a difference in the world, who can like herself, even if she is not perfect.

Thanks for writing your book. You've shown me that I am okay just as I am and that if I surround myself with the right people and fill my heart and mind with God's truth, I can be what God wants me to be.

For a long time I wanted to be like my dad, which made his words even more painful. But today his words are covered over, and I no longer want to be like him.

Keep telling teens to believe in themselves, who they are, and what they can become. If they don't believe, no one else will either.

Standing tall,
MaryAnn

MaryAnn began by changing the way she saw herself. Soon she felt that she had much to offer the world, and then she started acting on her feelings. She started to build good habits, and her whole life improved.

Others can help you, as MaryAnn said, but you have to decide to take those first, painful steps.

Not everyone turns his or her life around, however—just look at Vince. He'd used so many drugs that most of the time he just felt burned out—in fact, "Burnout" became his nickname. Most days Vince just floated through the halls or down the street, and the most he could think about was the moment. He had no plans for next week, next year, or the rest of his life.

Vince had a poor perception of himself. He couldn't remember a time when his mom and dad said, "I love you."

When Martin tried to tell Vince that God loved him, Vince wouldn't even listen. "What do you mean? No one could love a loser like me! Why should God?" The more Martin talked, the less Vince listened.

Vince's thoughts had trapped him—he'd begun to believe nothing good could happen in his life. And he'll be stuck in that trap until he begins listening to others who want to help.

Do you want to be like MaryAnn or Vince? The choice is yours.

Garbage In, Garbage Out

There's a well-known computer programming term called "GIGO." Those four letters stand for "garbage in, garbage out." You get out of a computer what you put into it. If you fill it with garbage, it will spit garbage back at you.

The people around you can fill you with hope— or dash it to the ground.

The same is true of your mind. You get out only what you put in. That is why I have told you repeatedly to hang around people who lift you up and encourage you. The people around you can fill you with hope—or they can dash it to the ground. Look at the harm MaryAnn's father did with a few words. For years she chose to believe what he said of her.

Be careful about listening to others or accepting the attitudes of those around you. What you become has a lot to do with what is fed into your mind. Friends and family will always have a big impact, but you must control what you believe and what you pay attention to.

Another area that influences what you think about yourself is the food you put in your mind. Do you read books that tell you life is hopeless? Do you listen to music that glorifies suicide or demeans human life? Do you "feed" your mind health food—or poison? Your mind can only act on the things you put in it, so feast on ideas and messages that encourage you to become your best.

Try exercising your mind with the following experiment. Put God's Word into your mind every night for a week, by reading from the Psalms or Proverbs for ten minutes right before you go to sleep. As you lay your head down on the pillow, silently repeat one of the verses or phrases from your reading. Do so until you fall asleep. Chances are you will sleep peacefully. After a few days, you should wake up more rested than you have in a long time.

Remember the last time you watched a frightening movie just before bed? You probably tossed and turned; maybe you woke up in the middle of the night, scared to death. That happened because you had fed yourself frightening stuff just before you went to sleep, and it came out in your mind.

If you influence your mind the same way—only with Scripture—you'll begin very soon to see results in the things that come *out* of your mind.

Reach Out

The ideas in this chapter have been designed to help you set personal goals that will be of value to you and others. Once you have your own goals in sight, you are ready to look at the things you can do to change the world. Now it's time to check out that goal. Is it worthwhile? Is it clear? Evaluate each of your goals by asking yourself:

- Do I have a clear goal?
- Can I describe that goal in a few sentences?
- Does it include other people?
- Does it encourage others to become the best they can be?
- Will it make me better, too?
- Is it based on sound ideas of right and wrong?
- Will it be good for my country or community?
- Will it cause people to stretch themselves and become better?

- Will God be pleased if this goal comes true?
- Will it further his purpose on earth?

How many yes answers did you have for each goal?

10–7: *You have well-defined goals. Learn how to put them into action in the next chapters.*

6–5: *Tune up your goals. You have some good ideas, but stop here and think about ways you can develop a better focus.*

4–3: *Read this chapter again and determine to spend more time putting its ideas into practice.*

2–0: *Don't get discouraged. It takes time to develop leadership habits and goals. Think about what you have already read and begin to come up with a few ways to improve your score. Are you thinking only of yourself? What can you do to change that?*

Discover a Vision of Right and Wrong

Few people in our society are able to stand for justice and consistently distinguish right from wrong. Do the goals you have fit that kind of vision? If not, you'll need to redirect them. Otherwise you are not holding out for the things you need to develop in your life—and encourage in others.

I've had many teens come up to me after I've spoken in their schools and thank me for being the only person who ever told them it's okay to be a virgin and that they are special when they save themselves for a husband or wife. I encourage them not to apologize for saying no to premarital sex. God says it's wrong. Saying no is in your best interest and the best interest of your date.

When I speak to parents, I challenge them to stand up for right and wrong by making their kids live it. I tell them to make booze off-limits—and not back down.

You will stand out from the crowd if you stand up for right against wrong, because so many people don't even know what those words mean. Develop your vision and share it with someone else, and you will be a leader.

CHECKPOINTS ✔

1. What would you like your future to look like? Write down personal, family, and spiritual goals. What would it take to make them happen?

_____

_____

_____

2. Use the space below to draw the road map (or treasure map) mentioned in this chapter (refer to page 116). Make it as detailed as you can.

3. What do you fill your mind with? List the three biggest influences on your thinking on the lines below (they can be people's names, rock groups, books, television shows, etc.). Are they usually positive or negative? Do you need to change them?

   _____

   _____

   _____

4. Have you developed a vision for yourself? Start by answering the five questions in the early part of this chapter. Think about yourself, what you would like to do with your life, and the tools you have in your life to accomplish them.

   _____

   _____

   _____

   _____

5. Using the guidelines in this chapter, draw up a plan that will help you put your goals into action. Do you need to learn some skills that will help you toward your goal? How can you do it?

   _____

   _____

   _____

The Extra Leadership Step

Goals, goals, goals! They keep popping up whenever we talk about leadership. I hope you haven't tired of hearing about them, because we're just about to talk about a very personal goal that could help you continue to be a leader for a long time.

"This leadership stuff isn't easy," Tanya complained. "Just when I thought I was getting a handle on it, I ran into a brick wall again. It seems as if I never really get there! When do I get to sit back and rest?"

While she looked for a break, Tanya missed out on one of the things that could have boosted her leadership skills into another league. The very skills she was having trouble with may have been the ones she needed to develop most.

What does a leader need to keep on doing in order to stay a leader? Keep on growing! Perseverance will keep you on the cutting edge of leadership.

Growth Ideas

I've noticed that people who lead by example don't slow down because they feel they've made it. They take the extra step and keep on accepting the challenge to become more than they are today.

One way they do that is by continually putting good, clean, pure, positive thoughts into their minds, to keep them going in the right direction. Just as a tree needs just the right amount of rain and sunshine each and every spring—and through the growing season—so do we.

Keep reading the Bible, because nothing will keep you growing like God's Word. Read it every single day for the rest of your life, because it has what you need to stay fresh and strong.

After many years of knowing God, I find it pretty easy to dig into his Word; I get excited about memorizing Scripture, I belong to Bible studies, and I share my faith pretty easily. Some people might think I really have it made spiritually.

But I still need to keep growing, because despite all I've learned, I could still take it all for granted. I could lie back on my laurels and feel that the Scripture reading and memorizing I did in the past will keep me strong today. But a tree can't live off last year's rain and I can't survive on last month's meals; I need to continually drink in God's Word, and keep feeding on what God says.

Recently I looked into my life and came up with ten things that will allow God to mold me and help me grow—and avoid spiritual starvation and dehydration. All of them will work in your life, too.

1. I force myself to stay in God's Word. Continually I look to God's Word for guidance. I enjoy the Book of Proverbs, which is filled with practical ways to do what God wants me to do and warnings about ways I should not do things. It shows me that if you do wrong, you will suffer consequences. Do the things God outlines

Perseverance will keep you on the cutting edge of leadership.

in this book, and you will experience beauty, joy, and peace.

2. I must challenge myself. Whether it's an exercise program, challenging myself to eat right, keeping New Year's resolutions, or continually learning communication skills, I have to keep growing and improving.

Do you remember the day my brother, Dale, challenged me by pointing out my pride? That's something

I have to work on again and again. Effective leaders keep improving themselves, so I had to admit that I needed to overcome my attitude.

3. I can keep my skills by ceaselessly practicing them. One of my favorite singers, Rich Mullins, told me he still practices on the piano for two hours a day. Though he has cut many albums, sells records all over the world, and is always being asked to do concerts, he keeps up with the basics.

If someone like that—who is at the top of his profession—needs to practice, so do I.

4. I need to try new things. All of us like to be comfortable—and change is never comfortable. In fact, it's one of the hardest things we can do. I try to step out of my comfort zone every so often, because change is healthy (and it's certain, too—we can't avoid it).

I challenge myself by looking at areas where I've done the same thing for a long time. (If you don't know where you need to change, ask your friends or family; they will give you some good ideas!) Trying new things not only expands my range of experiences and abilities, it also teaches me a lot about my fears and insecurities.

5. I stay accountable to others. I feel blessed because I have several people in my life who I am accountable to. Every week, I meet my pastor for lunch. We talk about what the Lord is doing in our lives and share the joys and pains of our ministries. In addition we challenge each other to walk by faith, to stand up for right, and never give in to evil. Almost every week I also meet with some friends who share this motto: Hate what God hates and love what God loves. We are honest and open with one another, and when one of them challenges me—with some way in which I wronged my wife, for example, or with insensitivity to someone at church—I own up to it.

My wife, Holly, is one of my greatest accountability experts. When you are really close to someone, you can't fool that person. Holly and I cannot lie to each other. She knows the areas in which I need help.

I am also accountable to my children. I cannot tell them one thing and do another—they always know it. They see the real me. If I act happy at church but turn ugly on the way home, they know it. If I sound good when I'm getting paid to give a talk, but yell at them for no reason, they see the inconsistency.

Taking challenges from others in a positive spirit can be hard, but it's also very important. So find someone you can be accountable to and learn how to take criticism gracefully.

6. *I write in my journal daily.* Each day I write something in my notebook. I write down things I've done well and ways I've goofed up. Then I follow it up with ideas about how I can make that better. It's my personal letter to the Lord in which I ask for his help, power, mercy, and love. Then I thank him for all he's done for me. I admit the places where I need help and ask him to mold and change me.

I challenge you to do this every day. Start today and make it a regular habit. If you miss a few days, don't agonize about it, just get back on target. When I remember to journal four to five times a week, my life runs much more smoothly.

7. *I must have a regular study program.* If I want to keep growing, I must not only set aside time to get into God's Word; I also need to learn in other areas. So I listen to wise people and read books from those who write from a godly perspective. I try to avoid people

who speak from anger or a false philosophy that will not serve the Savior.

8. I do what I should, even when I don't feel like it. Some things (like journaling or keeping in God's Word) are hard to keep up on a regular basis. It's a challenge to spend time on the things I need to do every day, but I try to disregard how I feel and do what I know is right.

9. I pray every day. Natural resources—like oil and coal—can power engines and furnaces; *super*natural resources—like prayer—can power the human soul. My strength comes from the Lord, so I spend time with him every day.

10. I exercise regularly. I need a good exercise routine at least four days each week to keep my heart going. Cardiovascular exercise is good for me. If this is a difficult discipline for you, find a friend who will work out

If you don't grow, you'll stagnate, and leaders who stay the same start becoming followers.

with you. Perhaps you can also tone up your bodies together by focusing on areas that need extra work.

If you don't grow, you'll stagnate, and leaders who stay the same start becoming followers. So challenge yourself to do the ten things I've outlined here. Push to become more today than you were yesterday; decide you'll be more tomorrow than you are today.

Growth will add so much to your life—and your leadership.

CHECKPOINTS ✔

1. Why is it important for leaders to grow? Can they grow only some of the time? Why or why not?

   _____

   _____

   _____

   _____

2. How many of the ten growth ideas are you already doing? Are you doing each on a regular basis? If so, how often? Do you need to improve in these areas? Make a plan that will help you keep growing.

   _____

   _____

   _____

3. How many of the growth ideas have you already tried but never succeeded in doing regularly? What stopped you from making them a habit? Find someone who has learned this habit and find out how it can become part of your schedule.

_____

_____

_____

4. Which of the growth ideas have you never tried? Has something stopped you from doing them? If nothing has stopped you, why haven't you made it a habit?

_____

_____

_____

Good Choice!

Right choices—don't you wish you could make them every day of your life? It's never as easy as it looks, is it? But making good choices is one of the keys to good leadership.

Like everyone else, leaders face decisions many times a day. But true leaders more often make good decisions—and stick to them. The only exception to that is that when they find they have made mistakes, they admit them quickly and develop a better plan.

Leaders are choosers, not losers. They don't let others lead them in the wrong direction for fear they will lose popularity. Instead, they carefully consider options and act on the one that has the best long-term gain.

Do you find it tough to make right choices? Many people do. We're going to look at some of the areas you may need help in, and you'll learn ways to take control of your decision-making processes.

Choice Advice

Begin to take control of your choices by making good decisions in the everyday things in your life. By practicing the small things first, you will learn to make wise choices without putting a lot on the line. Once you've gotten a handle on the little things, you'll begin to do better in larger decisions. So start practicing these things today, and you'll be surprised at how quickly you build up the power and skill to make even some of the larger decisions on the list.

- Choose your own meal off the menu when you go out with your friends, instead of asking what everyone else wants before you decide. Don't simply go along with the crowd.
- When it comes time to choose your classes for next year, pick out the subjects you really want to try, instead of copying your best friend's schedule.
- Decide today to say no to sex—even if you've said yes before.
- Choose what you will drink this weekend—and don't make it alcohol.
- Decide to live by wearing your seat belt—even if you are the only one in the car who does it.
- Determine how much studying you need to do to get a good grade on your tests, and spend that time hitting the books—no matter what else clamors for your time.

- Choose not to let your friends cheat off your test.
- Say no when a friend challenges you to steal your teacher's grade book.
- Talk to your parents when you feel pressure to do something wrong instead of relying on popular opinion about how you should handle it.
- Pick the people you want to share your life with, instead of going along with the crowd's opinion.

Make the decisions you know are right by starting with the small things first and working up to the big ones. If you can't say no to peer pressure about who should be your friend, start with getting a salad for lunch instead of a burger. But make some wise choices that will help you gain strength in decision making. Soon you will be able to stand for what you know is right in other areas, too. It just takes practice, so start today!

I know what it's like to go along with the crowd, because for many years I didn't make a lot of decisions on my own. As a result, I earned a lot of trouble and pain. Plenty of the scars I earned during those years still remain in my heart and memory.

But I also remember a time when I had enough courage to stand up for what was right. When I was fourteen, one of my friends who made a lot of bad choices decided to steal empty pop bottles from behind our local store to get the deposit money. It was a Friday night, and he wanted both of us to do it for kicks.

Instead, I chose to go home and watch TV with my parents. As I left, I thought I had made an incredibly boring choice for my weekend. But that boring and ordinary choice saved me from a lot of trouble.

Today, twenty-five years after my friend and I grad-uated from high school, he is headed for prison—and it's not for the first time! Those small larcenies bloomed into a life of crime.

Choices have consequences! You can avoid paying a high price if you become a wise chooser.

Sure, as a result of your decision, your life may seem "boring." You may be able to spend an evening home with your family and not have to worry about the impact drugs is having on your life. You will feel all the "boredom" of not having to worry if someone will figure out that you told him a lie and come after you for revenge. You might live in a house with mortgage payments you can afford and spend your time playing with your kids. Though you may not have the most admired job, you may go to one you love.

That kind of life can be yours if you establish the goal of making good decisions in four key areas of your life: the mental, physical, spiritual, and social areas.

Mentally

Do you consider what you read, think about, and listen to, instead of going along with the crowd? Here are some ways to avoid mental laziness.

- Force yourself to think each day. Spend a few moments each day thinking about the words that come from your mouth. Think about words that you spoke too quickly that you wish you could change. Determine to think first before speaking for the rest of the day. Think about how you could be a positive trendsetter at school by living out your beliefs.

- Read something each day that is not from one of your most enjoyable subjects. This will help your mind stay in shape and help it stretch.
- Look up words you don't know in the dictionary.
- Take your classes more seriously. Really apply yourself. Try for an A if you are now settling for a B. Don't let your mind become lazy or complacent. It sets the sails for your entire life.

Changing your life begins with changing your mind. Recently a boy shared with me that he had a problem with pornography. I knew what the problem was: He

No matter what your trouble, someone else has been through it, faced the challenge, and come out on the other side.

read it, looked at it, and spent time with it. "If you don't look at it, you won't think about it," I explained. "Choose not to look at it, and it won't be a problem."

Sure, if you walk into a store and your eye catches a glimpse of a pornographic magazine in a display rack, you can't control that. But you don't have to pick the magazine up and read it. You can even avoid that particular store in the future. You can control your actions—and your thoughts.

Right after sin tempts you, it's decision time. You have to ask yourself, Do I go along with the temptation or stand up and say no? The answer to that is all up to you. No one forces your hand. Since you will take the blame or the commendation for what you've done, it's all up to you.

Lots of teens make bad choices and then try to blame someone else for their mistakes. But that really isn't fair. When they faced that moment, it was their choice—and they made a bad decision. Once they chose, they couldn't really blame it on God, the devil, or family background, because none of them twisted those teens' arms. They each had an opportunity to go for the better choice.

For example, perhaps you've always been a worrier—you constantly feel fear about the future. "But that's something I can't control," you may say.

Ah, but you really can stop it! As soon as you understand that you control your thoughts, you can turn them around—if you are willing to put in the effort. Perhaps the real fact is that you don't want to change a life you've gotten used to. It would be too hard.

So instead of taking control of your life, you excuse yourself by blaming your mom and dad. "They never gave me any support," you say, as if that gets you off the hook.

Our families may hurt or handicap us, but the choices we make belong to us alone. Take responsibility for your own decisions. God has shown you the way, and you can't back out because you'd like an easier path or because, "I've always done it this way."

Physically

Do you choose to take care of your body and put the right things in it by eating a balanced diet? I hope so. After all, you do as much for your car, because you want it to run smoothly. You'll change the oil and fill it with gas whenever the tank nears empty so you don't get stuck somewhere. Well, you also need to treat your body to good food and exercise.

If you are drinking alcohol, you are not treating your body well. Instead, you're burning up some brain cells and toying with the possibility that you'll become addicted to a substance that destroys marriages, wrecks lives, and has ruined many dreams. You're headed for life as a loser, not a chooser.

When you don't pull your seat belt tight before you start the car, you are deciding not to take care of your body. If you have an accident, you'll have a much greater chance of being hurt or even killed.

Teens who decide to have premarital sex are sending their bodies and minds a deadly message.

Don't be like Melissa and Frank. When I talked to them, they told me they knew they would probably never marry, but they still wanted to have premarital sex.

"It's a beautiful thing," they told me. "Why are you trying to make it ugly and bad? God created it, didn't he?"

I agreed that he had, but I added, "He also gave the rules in which it is to be performed—within marriage.

"It's more than a physical act," I warned them. "It means more than a kiss and holding hands. God meant it to be a beautiful, loving, and bonding agent that holds a marriage together. He meant it to be used only in that unique and special relationship.

"Try putting a piece of tape on your arm four or five times, and you'll find that it begins not to stick; the hairs don't pull off your arm anymore. That's because the bonding agent is weakened. It's the same with anything you misuse—including sex."

When an authority from the Sex Education and Information Council told me I had forgotten to teach our kids that sex is a beautiful thing, I responded, "I don't need to teach junior high and high school kids how wonderful sex is. Their hormones are already telling them that.

"I'm not trying to teach people that sex is ugly; it is wonderful if it is done right—that means between a husband and wife within the bonds of marriage. But it is very painful and leaves lifelong scars if it isn't.

"Ask any man who has ever been unfaithful—me included—about the scars. Ask any woman who has given her body for money to tell how she feels about it. Those who are still doing these things will try to defend their actions; but those who were hurt and are now out of it will tell of emotional, physical, and spiritual scars that last a lifetime."

Maybe you don't have a problem in any of those areas. But you still may be treating your body as if it didn't matter.

I did that recently on a rafting trip. Forty of us from church spent a wild four days together. We drove from Michigan to West Virginia, and spent two days on the river relaxing and pulling lots of practical jokes. We ended with a fourteen-hour drive back home.

A few days after the trip, I still felt more irritable than I had in a long time. Any little thing set me off, and my stress level felt sky high. When my kids challenged anything I said, or if they got loud in the back of our van, I got all upset. Finally, I connected my attitude with the fact that I was burned out—that rafting trip had made me an emotional and physical wreck.

I'd forgotten one of my personal characteristics. If I don't get enough sleep, I can be a disaster waiting to happen.

Get to know yourself better. Learn that if you don't eat right, you will not do your best. When you don't get enough sleep and look after yourself, you will not serve the Lord in top form.

So care for your body and use it wisely—the way a leader should. If the crowd is staying up late, but you need more rest, get it. Go home early. Take a break from your friends. If they eat junk food, stand out and get the healthy meal that is right for you. Make sure that you take care of the body God has given you.

Spiritually

Every day you make important spiritual decisions, even if they seem quite small. It may not seem like such an exciting choice to pick up your Bible and memorize a verse so that it remains in your heart. But the impact of those few minutes could be to show you what God wants in your life. The verse you study in the morning may keep you from making a bad choice in the afternoon that would have affected your life for years.

You can start today to make small, wise choices that will influence you for the rest of your life. Do you regularly make time for a Bible study with other teens? Have you discipled a new Christian? When you go to church, do you carry a notebook and pen so you can take notes on the sermon? Do you spend time with your church youth group?

If you pay attention to spiritual things, you will make your life pleasing to God; you'll be pure for sure. Becoming part of something bigger than yourself will help you grow.

Someone may even be depending on the choice you make today. I've done it myself.

At the end of an assembly, I was counseling teens when I noticed about twenty were lined up to talk to me. I looked down in my hand, at the eight or nine gospel tracts I held. As I spoke, I was giving each teen a tract that challenged him or her to live for the Lord.

Just as I was ready to talk to the next person, a boy walked over from the other side of the gym. He had big, thick glasses and pimples. To put it kindly, he was not good looking. I didn't have to think hard to figure he wasn't the most popular student in his class.

After a few moments talking to him, I found out he'd only been in the school a few months.

"You're a Christian, aren't you?" he asked.

"Yes, I am. Thanks for noticing," I answered.

He surprised me by responding, "I sure did. God challenged me to give you these." In his hand were thirty more gospel tracts—different from mine, but bearing the same simple message of salvation.

I had to look up to heaven, thanking God for sending him. I'm not sure who he was; he could even have been an angel. But sometime—maybe that very morning—he had decided to bring those tracts to school, and because of that, I was able to touch the lives of more students. Though I may never learn his name, I will never forget his help just when I needed it.

Socially

Making good choices socially doesn't just mean spending time with your friends. Being in balance socially means more than that.

Do you choose to gain people skills? Can you talk to people you don't know well, smile at a stranger, and be gentle with someone who is hurting? When you meet someone new, do you ask her questions to show you are truly interested in her? Can you remember the name of someone you just met and tell him what he shared with you the next time you see him?

If you choose to gain people skills, others will be attracted to you. That's because we all need and like those who make us feel good about ourselves.

Effective leaders have people skills. But those abilities can be used for good—like inspiring a child to do his best—or bad—as with the leader who uses people for her own selfish means.

What are you doing with the social skills you have? Perhaps you are like Randy, who only thinks about himself. He's always talking about himself.

"What a know-it-all," Tasha complained after meeting Randy. "He can't let you get a word in edgewise!"

Is there hope for Randy? Yes, if he is willing to change. "He won't have many friends if he doesn't," Tasha commented.

If Randy gets lonely and begins to understand that he needs people skills, perhaps he'll be more willing to listen. Five years from now he could have lots of friends.

Or he could be even more lonely than he is today.

It's all up to him.

We are creatures of habit, and our habits don't change easily. If Randy keeps insisting on having the last word, many people will call him a loser. They'll avoid him whenever they can. But if he starts to care about others, focusing on the new habits he wants to have in his life, he need not stay in the same place.

When it comes to these four areas of your life, face the challenges you have and stand firm in the places where you are doing well. Avoid dirty stories or vulgar jokes by walking away from them. Decide not to be ashamed of Jesus Christ. With his help, you can make wise choices—and you will be a chooser, not a loser.

The Other Part of Choice

Do you understand how much the choices you make can influence others? It may be more than you think, because no matter how lonely you feel or how much you think others don't care, you *are* part of a larger world.

A teen who makes a choice to commit suicide may see it as the solution to a problem, but what was probably a final act caused by a temporary problem causes agony to family and friends—and even an entire community.

Your choices today *do* matter! So look for ways to solve—not avoid—problems. Look to God for help; nothing is too great for him. No matter what your trouble, someone else has been through it, faced the challenge, and come out on the other side. Use your creative mind and the wisdom of people who love you to find a way around or through any trouble you face.

When you do that, you will be showing your leadership ability by making wise decisions that will keep you and others in line with God's will.

> # With God's help, you can make wise choices— and you will be a chooser, not a loser.

I'm not saying you'll always be perfect. You may not make the wisest decisions since Solomon. You may still get confused. Even seasoned leaders blow it on occasion. They have bad days when they make poor choices, but most of the time they have the strength for the hard choices. They have their spirits under God's control, and they try to make wise decisions in the mental, physical, and social areas of their lives.

Such people have an overwhelming goal: Someday they hope to hear God say to them, "Good choices!"

CHECKPOINTS ✔

1. What makes it so difficult to make hard choices? Think of a tough decision you've had to make.

Why did you have trouble with it? What influenced you to decide the way you did? Did you make the right choice? If not, how could you have handled it better? What influences should not have swayed you?

_____

_____

_____

2. Do you sometimes feel as if your life is boring? Are you avoiding trouble because you are saying no to things that could cause trouble in your life? Does your life need to be a little more boring?

_____

_____

_____

3. Name the four areas in which you need to make wise decisions. Rate yourself overall in each, choosing a number from one to ten. Now identify areas you could improve in. Take each one and ask yourself, "What is my problem? How can I start solving it?"

_____

_____

_____

_____

4. Have you ever tried blaming other people for your wrong choices? Why? Did it solve your

problem? What happened to the problem? How
did you solve it?

_____

_____

_____

5. What kind of people skills do you have? What
   areas do you wish you were better in? Why? Do
   you know someone who has that kind of skill?
   Ask for help in learning how to deal with people
   in that area.

_____

_____

_____

6. When have you seen how your choices influenced others? Think of times when they have
   had an impact on your family, friends, or the
   community. Were you proud of the results?
   Why or why not? Did you expect your actions
   to have that kind of impact? What did this
   experience teach you?

_____

_____

_____

Rights or Wrongs?

I will never forget the first time I met Josh McDowell. In a few minutes, that man taught me a lot about leadership.

This Christian speaker was about to lead two hundred leaders in a "Why Wait?" campaign seminar. In it, he would help us discover more ways to reach teens with the message that they could wait for sex until they married. But before the seminar began, the "man in charge" grabbed our bags and carried them to our rooms. Josh introduced us and gave us each a welcoming handshake. For twenty-four hours straight, with a smile on his face, he did it all—and at the end, Josh still ran up the stairs two at a time!

Later, I asked him why he made such an effort when he didn't have to.

"My hero washed feet," he responded, reminding me of the way Jesus humbled himself before his disciples just before his death on the cross.

Josh was telling me that leadership is synonymous with servanthood.

In fact, since then, I've learned that there is no more surefire way to stand out for the Lord than by serving others.

Making Real Leadership Choices

The concept of servant leadership isn't the most popular one. If you buy into that idea, you will be going against the flow. Following in Jesus' footsteps by giving up your rights won't please a lot of folks. That's because we live in an era when most of the world denies God's right to their lives.

Out there on the street, it's popular to demand your own rights. You hear testimony to that fact every day:

"It's my right!"
"I plead the fifth!"
"I'll do what I please with my body!"
"No one is going to tell me what I can and cannot do!"

You've seen signs of this on television—and maybe in your own school—when the subject of abortion comes up.

Many women cry out: "It's my body!" "It's my right!" "It's not a good time for me to have a child, so I'm going to abort it!"

How many of these people have already asked the questions: What is right? What would God want me to do? Will God hold me accountable for this action?

Not many, I'd say.

The "I'll have it my way" mentality has distorted the abortion question for many Americans.

The Wrong Rights

People who get hung up on rights have missed out on one of the great paradoxes of Scripture: When you hold on to your rights, you actually give up much more than you gain. "For anyone who keeps his life for himself shall lose it; and anyone who loses his life for me shall find it again" (Matt. 16:25).

I'm not trying to tell you to become a doormat, but I am asking you to remember that your right to do what you want will influence other people. The decisions you make could negatively affect lives—maybe even your own.

Look, for example, at a girl who gave up a baby to abortion. "I thought having a child was inconvenient," Lisa explained. "People wanted to know how I would care for her. So I gave in to the pressure and had an abortion.

"But no one told me," she cried, "about the pain I would feel after that decision."

No one told Lisa about post-abortion trauma—the emotional impact of knowing you killed your own child.

No one tells thousands of teens each year that the instant gratification they get while playing Nintendo by the hour won't get them employed.

No one tells many newlyweds that to be selfish and think only from one point of view is a surefire road toward divorce.

Each one of us has the right to be wrong. But to live by way of the wrong rights will surely have negative consequences in the end.

Fighting for the Right Rights

It is a natural tendency—perfectly human—to stand up for your own rights, and even to justify wrong behavior by appealing to your "rights." But if you are going to live as a leader and be your best, you must fight that tendency. Rather than going with the flow, you will encourage others to recognize absolutes. Instead of saying there are no definite moral standards, avoiding the idea of right versus wrong, and denying that God even exists, you will choose to stand up for unpopular things like a child's right to life.

Grabbing the "rights" society seeks will make you wrong before God. You may become successful, rich,

When you hold on to your rights, you actually give up much more than you gain.

and even famous, but you will not be happy and content in this life—or the next.

I learned something about contentment through the example of my friend Bob Lemieux, one-time general manager for a professional soccer team.

One year, Bob's team went to the Soccer Bowl in Washington, D.C. He cheered them on from the stands as he watched the game with his daughter, Nikki, who had leukemia.

Near the end of the game, when the team was far behind, Nikki surprised him by saying, "Daddy, I'm very sorry. I know this is the saddest thing for you, because to you the most important thing in the world is winning this particular game."

Those sentences stopped Bob in his tracks. His daughter's words made him realize he'd placed too much emphasis on his career—and this game in particular. His whole life had become wrapped up in it; for hours and hours he trained, motivated, and inspired his team. But while he poured his life into those men, he was missing out on the life of his ill daughter. "Who knows how long I will have her?" he asked himself.

So Bob decided to move back to his hometown in Michigan, leaving behind Miami and the excitement of professional sports. He refused to put his "right" to a career he loved before the rights of his daughter to have a father's love.

Bob's decision has been worth it. Today he knows his children well. Instead of spending time with the team, he has made his family his team. He founded an organization that fights for the rights of youngsters by seeking justice for them and supporting family values. Almost every night, Bob spends time at home, with the family members who once rarely saw him.

Leaders know what's most important in life, and they can make a career second to the people they love. As a result of that choice, their hearts remain whole; they don't lose their families. Instead, they can reach out to the hurting people who need to see the example of a strong family built on faith in God.

Beyond Gusto

There's more to reach for in life than the gusto a long-running beer commercial once promised. A better goal is the clean, secure feeling of being friends with your Creator. When you know God and seek to live for him, you can look yourself in the eye and admire what you see. You'll be a person of integrity, because you'll live up to your principles, and what you say will be what you do.

"None of that is easy!" you may point out.

You're right! Nothing special and wonderful is easy—and that goes for being a person of integrity. You'll need the wisdom of the ages on your side to keep you from going the way of the multitudes—the way of mediocrity.

But when you take that road, you will become free to be your best. Someday your spouse will brag of your integrity. When your word is your bond, you will probably never face a divorce, a custody battle, or the tear-filled eyes of your children, who only see you every other weekend.

Your son or daughter will hold your hand tight and be proud to walk through the mall with you. Whether your child is in the first or seventh grade, she will love and trust you, because you are the only parent on the block who keeps all his promises. Your neighbors will envy you, and your friends' eyes will light up, because they feel proud to know you and be called your friend.

Employers may want you to work for them, because you will stand out from the rest. You could be offered raise after raise, and promotion after promotion.

Leaders know what's most important in life.

Does all this sound too good to be true? It doesn't have to be. God truly wants to flood you with his love and blessings. He wants to be your close, dear friend. And he will speak to you, showing you the safest way to travel through life.

How can you have all these things? Simply choose what is right and don't be caught up in being noticed and demanding your rights at any cost. It's the greatest choice of all—one with many benefits.

CHECKPOINTS ✔

1. What rights do you hear others demanding? What ones have you demanded? Have your ideas about your rights changed from reading

this chapter? If so, how does your thinking differ?

_____

_____

_____

2. What does it mean to be a servant? How can being a servant make a difference in the choices you make?

_____

_____

_____

3. How have you acted as a servant? What has kept you from being a better servant?

_____

_____

_____

4. What can make you a better servant? Identify people who act as servants in your life. Talk to them about the convictions that allow them to serve others. Then write down some ideas that could help you become a better leader in this area.

_____

_____

_____

5. Is God your best friend? If not, ask him to become that. What do you need to do for that

to happen? From the chapters you have already
read, draw up a plan that will help you obey
him daily.

_____

_____

_____

Leaders or Followers?

One of the things that separates leaders from the people who go along with the crowd is the way they think.

Instead of accepting the "party line" from the cool kids in town, leaders can set their own agenda, goals, and lifestyle. They can make decisions for themselves, based on the best ideas.

Leadership Thinking

Do you take charge of your life? Do you believe that you are in control of your actions? If so, you have already begun leadership thinking.

Here are eleven thought concepts that make leaders stand out.

1. Leaders realize that the decisions they make and the efforts they put forth determine what happens to them. They take responsibility for their own actions by not blaming life, fate, or anyone else for their choices.

You won't often hear these sentences come from leaders' mouths:

"I always have bad luck!"

"Well, what can you expect? Look at her environment."

"My parents made me this way. I can't change that."

"It's not my fault."

"Nothing good ever happens to me."

Followers blame luck, circumstances, or other people for the challenges they face. Leaders know that God did not make us robots; he created people who can choose. We can determine the good, the bad, and the ugly by what we put into our lives. There will always be a choice.

Even when you have made a bad choice, you can turn it around. Countless teens tell me they have made the bad choice of having premarital sex. But after making that first bad choice, they have decided to hold out for a marriage partner.

We call these teens secondary virgins. They have accepted God's forgiveness and put themselves back on his potter's wheel, where he can mold them and shape them in his character. Looking to him to give them the courage to stick to that decision and believe they are worth waiting for, they have faith that even if they did fail once, they have only one mistake under their belt. When they meet their spouses, they can say,

"No, I'm not a virgin. I made a mistake. But God gave me the ability to say no, and for the last several years I have saved myself for you." Their spouses will know they can be trusted to be faithful, because they have stood for what is right.

I encourage you to start your marriage on this kind of strong foundation. If you have failed, turn around and do things God's way. Ask his forgiveness—and you will be part of a few strong people who have done that. Set yourself up as a person who is willing to lead with integrity. Leading with integrity doesn't mean never making a mistake; it means developing a lifestyle that shows you can be trusted.

I am sick of hearing people excuse themselves with, "I did it because it was easy." I'm tired of hearing, "Everyone else was doing it!" People who think that way have fallen for Satan's lie. Millions believe it.

Sin is commonplace. But people who encourage you to sin will never tell you of the pain and heartache it causes. You won't hear stories of their broken dreams and lives.

A friend of mine, Jacob Aranza, challenges young people to be ready to have their spouses ask, "Did you wait for me? Are you a virgin?" When he asks that question, many teens have to hang their heads in shame.

I know what that feels like. I know the pain that goes with the lifestyle that says yes to sex outside of marriage. And I also know that each time I sinned, it was my decision. I was not powerless, I was not forced to do wrong. But when I admitted those things to myself, I saw that, just as I had the power to choose evil, I could choose the opposite! I could decide to stand out from the crowd. And I did.

If you have never given in to one of nature's strongest desires—premarital sex—don't. If you have given in, start again by admitting your mistake, asking God's forgiveness, and deciding to turn over a new leaf.

Let the guilt and hurt you feel work for good by keeping you in the right way. Don't hang onto that pain for a lifetime. But say, "Because of this feeling that I do not like, I will not do it again. I will be pure and live up to God's standard."

Leaders understand that many of the best things in life don't pay off immediately.

Make choices for good, instead of blaming circumstances and the people around you. Realize that whatever your life is today, it became because of the decisions you've made. Turn around the bad choices and start making good ones by letting God take control of your life. Follow him day by day, and you can remain in those positive choices.

2. Leaders see through manipulation. Followers believe the TV ads that tell them they will become glamorous, healthy, wealthy, wise, and popular if they use a product. When an ad man tells them, "All you need to do is buy this," they fall under his spell.

Leaders know that such people do not have their best interests at heart. They understand that "instant success" is a myth. Buying advertisers' beer, using their toothpaste, or getting a loan on some wheels will not fulfill those promises—and leaders know it.

When a soap opera hands out the message that you can go to bed with that sexy someone and have a happy life, leaders know that is not reality; they recognize that kind of irresponsibility as the path to disease, low self-esteem, abortions, divorces, and wrecked lives. Followers eagerly accept the falsehood that people can do as they please and everything will come out all right, just as it did at the end of the show.

We need to look deeper than surface messages. Life has its rewards, but it also has its pains.

3. Leaders see cause and effect at work in their lives. Followers look to escape the results of their actions. "If you do the crime, you do the time" is a saying leaders understand. They know that risk-taking with wrongdoing isn't worth it.

Followers seldom—if ever—think ahead to the consequences of their actions. When they get caught, they blame it on someone who spilled the beans, or figure it just wasn't their day. They don't accept the fact that they brought it on themselves by the things they did or said or the people they hung around with.

Remember, every action has an equal and opposite reaction. When you do something, good or bad, something of the same type will result. Good actions bring good reactions; bad actions bring bad reactions.

4. Leaders can put off pleasure until tomorrow. Followers look for instant gratification. They spend their allowance as soon as they get it, because saving "takes too long." They see no point in practicing free throws because, they explain, "the coach never lets me play anyway." Some of them refuse to enter college because they want to start making money *now*, not four years from now.

Leaders, however, understand that many of the best things in life don't pay off immediately. The person who studies hard when he could play ball may eventually reap benefits—like good grades, prestige, and scholarships. The teen who painfully practices the piano on a day when she could be in the pool may someday enjoy fame as a fine pianist. The youth who puts off sexual involvement until marriage will probably enjoy a healthy relationship with his spouse.

Many Americans want to enjoy a lifestyle before they have put in the effort. Mass media has given us the message that instant gratification is our right, and we have fully bought into that concept.

How many young people leave college, expecting instantly to have the level of income and lifestyle their parents enjoy? After all, I'm smarter than Mom and Dad, they may think. So I should be able to do it in a snap.

What they don't realize is that it took their parents thirty to forty years to achieve their current lifestyle. When it doesn't come that easily, the young person may feel disillusioned.

Put forth the effort today, pay the price, and put off gratification until tomorrow. Wisdom and hard work will help you achieve your goals. You'll get them, not through a wishbone, but through backbone.

Meeting your goals takes special inside stuff. But don't worry—you've got it, or you wouldn't be reading this book.

5. Leaders go within; followers go without. Leaders search inside themselves for peace and happiness, instead of always expecting others to make their day. For example, they look for faith in God and reinforce that by reading the Bible, spending time in prayer, and worshiping with others. But good things don't have to happen on the outside in order for them to feel good inside. They have an inside strength that pulls them through bad times.

Followers believe that if circumstances don't come out just right, if they don't do well on the test, get what they want, and have things happen the way they planned, they have the right to get hurt, depressed, and spend their time dwelling on how everyone hates them.

You can't do that, because life isn't painless. And leaders know it!

I want you to feel great inside, because you know God's love. When you feel capable and know you have the ability to make good choices because God has a plan for you and you want to follow it, you can experience an inner strength you never thought possible. When fellowship with the Creator of the universe means more to you than owning the world's silver and gold, you can feel a peace so wonderful, strong, and indestructible that you can't describe it.

People long for that kind of strength and peace—some change husbands or wives four or five times, just looking for it. Many change jobs to find it. Others change their convictions or beliefs in search of it. But if you know Jesus, you have it right inside you now. Realize that the Lord is only a prayer away, and his fellowship gives you a peace that passes understanding.

So don't depend on circumstances, people, and the actions of others to make you happy. Depend on the Lord of the universe—Jesus Christ.

6. *Leaders don't want others to do for them what they can do for themselves.* Those who don't lead encourage others to do for them, even though they could do those things for themselves. But a leader will not let his father or mother take on a chore he could do for himself, whether it is making the painful phone call to apologize for what he's done wrong or confronting a friend about careless or immoral behavior.

A follower encourages others to take on his responsibilities and cries if no one will do it. People like this are known as whiners when they are children, and as adults they earn a reputation as lazy people who enjoy using others. Integrity is not part of their inside stuff.

If you are the kind of person I think you are—the kind God wants you to be—remember that God will not do for us what he has given us the power to do. Though he will help us when we need him, he won't take over and take charge, allowing us to become like little babies.

He won't:

Do your studying or planning
Make apologies for you
Do your praying for you

He gave you the ability to do all those, so get on with them.

Don't wimp out and let someone do what you can do yourself. Think instead about bad habits you could be acquiring and stop them in their tracks. Start good habits by taking on responsibility today.

7. Leaders organize, while followers agonize. Do you look at your life and ask, How can I get organized? Do you follow that up with, Okay, let's make a list and follow it! How should I change my behavior? Do things differently? Improve what I've done before?

Or do you agonize over what has happened in your life? Instead of organizing for improvement, followers worry and complain. They live miserably, because their lives don't change. When asked to explain what happened, they fret, "It happened that way with my parents." Or "My dad said it would happen that way." Or even, "My teachers warned me about this, and it's happening to all my friends, too. So you can't blame me!"

Leaders will choose to get organized and do things differently, once they realize something must change.

Don't let yourself agonize when you only need to get organized!

8. Leaders take responsibility; followers blame. Over the past ten years I've spent a lot of time in prisons—talking to the inmates. I've learned one thing from them: Most people don't take responsibility for their mistakes. A handful of the prisoners have admitted they were doing time for something they did. But 99 percent claim it's not their fault; they blame it on someone else. I've heard every excuse you can think of—and every one focused the blame somewhere else.

Others do it, too. Adults who were fired blame the factory, the firm, or the world. But when you look at their history, you can frequently see that this pattern has repeated itself over and over again.

When loved ones keep repeating the same message about your life, listen. When people who care for you tell you that you need to change, pay attention. It doesn't mean you have to listen to anyone who persistently says one thing. If someone tells you that booze is good and won't hurt you or that safe sex is all right, don't go along with those ideas. But listen carefully to constructive criticism from your parents, teachers, or other loved ones—the people who have the most interest in your life.

9. *Leaders recognize and listen to people who have their best interests at heart.* Followers listen to anyone who is popular, but leaders have more discernment.

I challenge you to take advice from wise people who want the best for you. If you see that a friend can't control her own life, don't seek out her advice on how to run yours. Don't listen to people who tell you to follow them into trouble and a life that leads nowhere.

Instead, consciously choose the people who can help you—and do it daily. Find those who do good stuff in their families, at school, and in the community. Watch them live it out and learn from them.

10. *Leaders have significant other people in their lives.* At-risk kids can often be recognized by the lack of supportive people they have in their lives. Successful people have at least one significant other—a teacher, parent, relative, youth pastor, or neighbor—who has had an impact on their lives. Most successful people will tell you somebody came along at just the right time, just when they were ready to reach for success. At-risk kids often have missed out on this important boost.

Have you been ready to hear the people who have challenged you to become the best you can be? If not, maybe that's why you have not heard the message.

Many significant others have touched my life. Years ago, Don Davies, my Dale Carnegie instructor, told me I had a speaking talent. Well, at first I didn't believe him. Over and over, for three years, he repeated that message, and I finally began to trust him. I realized that I had nothing to lose by following his advice.

I started acting on the belief that what Don had seen in me was true. Because I put it to use, it became my lifestyle.

When I planned on quitting college, a counselor named Chuck Holland told me that he needed me at that school to help others and touch lives. After a while, I believed him—and today I go into schools and teach teachers how to touch lives. To reach kids, I answer letters, pray for them, and talk to them when they come to see me. Significant others touched my life, and I'm trying to do the same for people I meet.

I haven't had a significant other in my life, some teens are thinking as they read this. My mom and dad didn't give me all those positive things, and no one else has seemed to care.

Perhaps your parents have struggled with their own problems and had little time to encourage you. But you can still become a leader by going out and finding a significant other. Find an adult you can admire—someone who has wisdom, integrity, and character, who is living the way you would like to someday. Tell that person of your need for a mentor. Get the help you need to secure your future.

Though Don and Chuck came into my life unrequested, I have also searched out others who could help. I look for people all the time who are wise, at peace, and walking close to the Lord. Then I tell them I want to learn from them.

Jim Roscheck, my golf instructor, is such a man. I saw how he worked with people. He showed a true concern for me personally. When I felt sick, he showed he cared. When something good happened to me, he called or asked me to tell him about it the next time he saw me.

I don't care how much a person knows until I know how much he cares. Jim does care, so I can learn from him. When he works with me on my golf swing, he doesn't just tell me what I'm doing wrong. He builds on my successes. First he told me about the importance of having the right posture and placing my hands properly. Then he began working on my feet (which were jumping all around), my wrists, and my back swing.

I remember one day when I hit a perfect drive. "Now that's the way I want to do it all the time!" I exclaimed.

"Great shots will cost you more," Jim warned.

"Name your price!"

"It's awful expensive," he said, before finally naming the price: "Practice!"

"Anything but that! Not that—oh, no—not practice!" I replied.

I went to Jim because I liked his expertise *and* the fact that he really cared about me. But he didn't let all that caring stop him from providing something else I needed: the truth. He told me where I was going wrong, so I could have a better score.

Jim has had a significant role in my life. I'm hitting the ball a lot better now.

11. Leaders do what is right; followers want their rights. People who understand that moral absolutes—right and wrong—exist can become leaders. They know God was here first, and he laid down the rules we need to live by.

Followers want things to go their way. Even if they don't have much to say, they want others to listen to them and follow in their path. They expect people to respect them, even when they live a life no one can admire. They expect friendship, even when they haven't been a friend to anyone else. Instead of facing problems squarely, they seek to avoid them.

Being a leader means you are more than a smooth talker, or someone with charisma. True leaders lead from their hearts. They follow ideas and people that are worth standing up for.

When leaders who are worth following make mistakes, they realize that God allows us to do that—and to pay the consequences ourselves.

True leaders don't seek to be noticed as much as they seek to notice others. They don't ask to be served and recognized, but are willing to do those things for others. True leaders listen more than they talk and understand that others have feelings, too.

These eleven characteristics of leadership thinking can have a powerful influence on your life, because how you think directs your actions—and your life. If this pattern of thinking is new to you, begin to practice it. Toss out the old ideas and replace them with life-building ideas for your future.

Consciously choose the people who can help you—and do it daily.

I pray that deep down in your soul you will learn to do something because it is good, because it will build discipline in you, because you will be able to understand yourself and God much better. God needs disciplined, loving people who he can lead, and he is the ultimate resource that helps us become all we can be and enables us to lead others out of despair.

CHECKPOINTS ✔

1. Review the eleven qualities of leaders described in this chapter. Do you have any of them? If so, which ones? (List them below.) Which do you feel you most need to develop? Start planning ways you can begin to make them part of your life.

   _____

   _____

   _____

2. Do you understand that much of what happens in your life results from the actions you take and the decisions you make? If you have a hard time accepting that, is it because you do not care to face the facts? Why is it hard to accept?

   _____

   _____

   _____

   _____

3. What people support you as a leader? Challenge
    your desire to be a leader? Provide you with
    good role models? How can people help you or
    hinder you as you seek to lead?

    _____

    _____

    _____

4. Has anyone ever told you that you had a talent
    you couldn't see in yourself? How did you
    respond? Have you ever wanted to try some-
    thing new and excel at it? What has kept you
    from developing these talents? Begin today to
    work on a plan that will help you develop an
    ability you could use to help others or enrich
    the world.

    _____

    _____

    _____

Tough Times in Leadership City

When we talk about standing out, it not only means standing out from the crowd; it also refers to standing out *against* something.

Sometimes that "something" is tough times.

As you've read this book, you've never seen the words, "This will be easy and pleasant. You will always enjoy being a leader, and you will have plenty of fun each day." That's because I would be lying if I said that. I'd be selling you a fairy tale.

Everyone has tough times in life—and leaders often face more than followers. Stand for something you believe in, and you will always get some attention. Not all of it will be pleasant.

Strong Medicines

When you face the tough times, you'll need strong medicines to get you through. So I've developed a prescription that will heal your hurts, keep you going, and bring you energy. Here are the ingredients.

1. Remember that you are performing God's will. Facing opposition is easier when you know why you are doing it. If you stand up against drinking, and people make fun of you or argue with you, keep in the back of your mind that you are doing God's will by keeping other teens from pursuing an addictive lifestyle that will hurt them forever. You are making your Creator happy.

And, though taking a strong stance for right may be inconvenient or difficult, it is far better than disappointing your Best Friend, Jesus. Who do you want to please more than your Lord and Savior?

2. Focus on the fact that right will win in the end. As the kind of leader God wants you to be, you will stand up for truth in a world of counterfeits. But that will not exempt you from facing tough times. But realize, too, that being on the popular side is not important—being on the right side is. And, very often, you will be rewarded for a courageous stand.

I know this happens because it happened in my own life, when I spoke at a school in a major western city.

Anyone who has heard me speak knows that I am not ashamed of my faith. When I teach people about their self-worth, it is vital that I let them know that they are not a mistake, but a well-planned act of God. I share with students creatively and tactfully, usually using a lot of humor.

This day I knew that (though I had been invited there by two large groups of students) a lot of corporate people from several major companies would be listening. I also had learned that one company was looking for a speaker to sponsor. If they sponsored me, they would pay my fee and all my expenses, as long as I used their name and said something positive about them.

That great opportunity placed me on the horns of a dilemma. After the first session of speaking, someone reported that two or three teachers had objected to my "preaching." (I had used three or four illustrations that used the words *God* or *Creator*.) So I decided to leave these out when I spoke before the corporate people.

Halfway through my speech, when I had left out God, I learned something valuable about myself: I am not happy when I don't follow my heart. I wasn't doing what was right, and I knew it.

I am teaching kids in a difficult and treacherous time, I decided. If I am to be persecuted for implying that

Everyone has tough times in life—and leaders often face more than followers.

there is a Creator, then so be it. I had to be true to my faith. God had placed it in my heart, and I had to speak out, no matter how much pressure I felt against it.

Right in the middle of my talk, I stopped and told everyone how I felt. I shared that I did not like having to leave out part of my talk.

"I'm going to give you the rest of my talk just as it usually is. I will never again leave any of it out.

"If I don't get the sponsorship, so be it, because I have learned I have to be true to myself. I do not feel as if I am preaching. I feel I am telling you a minimal amount of what you need to reach your goals, fight peer pressure, and raise your self-worth. Those are the things I have been asked to instill in you today."

The rest of the talk followed my usual pattern.

At the end, I received a standing ovation. Thirty or forty students told me I was the first one who told them they were special enough to say no to premarital sex, drugs, alcohol, and tobacco. They thanked me for giving them courage to stand up when other teens mock them for being virgins or not partying hearty, like the rest. Some shared the persecution, pain, and suffering they experience for their stand. Then they thanked me for providing examples of people who showed them how to be true to themselves.

After that assembly, I went to a luncheon with the corporate sponsors. I spoke to one man who had sat in the front row, and I asked if there was a chance the company could sponsor me.

"Absolutely," he responded. Then he told me of some of the wishy-washy speakers he had heard, who gave kids nothing but fluff. Though they made teens laugh, these speakers avoided attacking the issues.

"Obviously," this executive said, "I don't know about the future of us working together, but you are exactly what we are after. Never, ever let up. Always stick to your guns. Stay true to yourself, and keep challenging kids the way you did today. You really touched some lives."

I discovered that remaining true to the faith God gave me made others treat me with respect. When I stood up for him, I could stand out from the multitudes. Right won in the end—and I had the bonus of gaining the good opinion of some adults and touching teens' lives.

Ultimately I have confidence that God's way will win because I have read the entire Bible. Many times as I share my faith with others, they don't like what I have to say, or they make fun of me. When I feel discouraged from receiving such abuse, I remember that the Book of Revelation says Satan will be cast forever into the eternal lake of fire, along with everyone who serves him. All the demons that tempt me today, day in and day out, will be with him, while I will live forever with God. That promise gives me hope.

Though you may not feel as if you are winning the spiritual war when others make fun of you, remember—this is just one battle. When you stand on God's side, you will win in the end.

3. *When times get tough, refocus on your blessings.* On those hard days, when you feel as if you simply cannot go on, make a blessed list. Write down all the blessings God has given you.

Blessed Beyond Words

When you write your blessed list, don't forget to include some of the following things.

- Eyes
- Ears
- Your heart

- Living in a free country
- The ability to breathe
- Clear mental abilities
- Your physical abilities
- Good health
- Family members who love you (name them, one by one)
- Friends who care deeply about you (name each)
- Other people who believe in you and would never harm you (name each one)
- Your special abilities (include musical talents, sports abilities, your sense of humor, and so on)

By the time you finish this, you should have fifty or sixty things listed. Look at each and realize the priceless gifts God has given you. No amount of money in the world could pay for them all. Once you have understood how blessed you are, you can focus on the beautiful things in life, not the tough time you face today.

4. Make a success list. When you face goals that seem impossible, it's time to look at how far you've come. Today, even if you are not in trouble, write out a list of things at which you've succeeded in the past.

Successful Living

When you spell out your successes, keep some of these in mind. The time you:

- Read that entire book, even though it was hard to do
- Got an A on a paper
- Hit a home run
- Baked a cake by yourself
- Regained a nearly lost friendship
- Lost ten pounds

- Made it through your track class
- Won the spelling bee
- Helped a friend who was hurting
- Became a reading buddy for a younger student
- Had the courage to ask a question in class
- Convinced a friend not to drink

You've been successful at many things. Spend time remembering them, and write them down. When you hit tough times, encourage yourself by reviewing them. Then you'll be able to say to yourself, It was hard for me to accomplish this, but I stuck it out. With God's help, I can get through this, too.

Perhaps some young people in Moscow have been looking at their success list. In August 1991, they had a great success in overthrowing Communism. Twenty-five young freedom fighters stood arm-in-arm before the Russian parliament building, while tanks headed toward them. As the tanks drew closer, fear swept the city, but this handful of young people stood firm, defending their newfound freedom.

Soon others joined them, and fifty—then a hundred—stood out. Soon thousands of people carrying bricks, steel rods, rocks, tree limbs—anything they could use to defend themselves from the tanks—stood together.

Their leader, Boris Yeltsin, appeared, calling for courage and unity in this showdown of "right against wrong."

Communism fell that day. Even the efforts of party members to overthrow the Russian leader have not been successful.

Perhaps it's because those young people could look back to a success list that read: Stood out courageously against Communism.

Perhaps you have never had to lay your life on the line for your freedom, but you've had your own successes—some of which you can't even remember anymore. It's been so long since you learned to skip, jump rope, say the alphabet, write, ride a bike, talk, and walk. But all of them took some struggle. You had to spend time learning them, and it wasn't always easy. Though you can't remember when you accomplished these things, I want to remind you, so you can remember that life hasn't been easy every day. Grow when times get tough by hanging in there.

5. Ask the advice of friends and family. Ask for suggestions from your mom and dad and friends. Let them help you discover new ways to accomplish your goal when you are bogged down in problems. Even if they can offer no new ideas, you may receive their encouragement, moral support, or personal assistance.

Solomon revealed his famous wisdom when he wrote, "Two can accomplish much more . . . If one falls, the other pulls him up . . . And one standing alone can be attacked and defeated, but two can stand back-to-back and conquer; three is even better, for a triple-braided cord is not easily broken" (Eccles. 4:9–12).

Get input from the people who care about you; let them help. As you tap into their enthusiasm, you may find yourself with a new vision of yourself. I can do this, you may decide. That encouragement may be all you needed to triumph.

6. Read encouraging stories about great leaders. Discover how they have overcome difficult times by hanging in there.

Read stories of other teens who have accomplished great things, so you know you can do them, too. I was recently inspired by the story of Lori Cox, who lives in Scottsdale, Arizona. She got enough signatures on a petition to regain the privilege of saying the Pledge of Allegiance in her school. Today they have this freedom because she took the effort to do it.

All your inspiration need not come from books. If you have a neighbor you admire because she accomplished something great, ask her how she did it. Find out what kept her going, what her secret was, and how she found extra energy when her spirit sagged.

Learning from what others have gone through will give you much strength.

Being on the popular side is not important—being on the right side is.

7. Depend on God. When the going gets tough (and it's even tough just to get going), you can do it if God is on your side. He has not given you the vision to lead for nothing. He will not close a door without opening a window. When you cross the water, he will never let you be destroyed on the rocks. Though you may have an uphill climb, he will be with you all the way.

Turn to God. Energize and strengthen yourself by renewing your mind. In the next chapter we will look at some ways you can do that.

You can grow during the tough times if you don't give up. Though it may hurt for a little while, the skills you learn and the changes in your character will be worth it in the end. God is making you into the leader he needs tomorrow, and he has promised never to leave you or forsake you.

Hold on during the tough times; they won't last forever.

CHECKPOINTS ✔

1. Why do you think it is harder to be a leader than a follower?

   _____

   _____

2. Why do you think people still want to lead?

   _____

   _____

3. Name some of the "strong medicines" that can help you. Have you made out a blessed list? If not, start writing it now.

   _____

   _____

   _____

   _____

4. How can focusing on other people's successes help you when you face tough times? Write down the story of someone whose ability to overcome has inspired you. What qualities did you admire in that person's life? How has it influenced the way you live?

_____

_____

_____

_____

Tough Faith
in Tough Times

After I spoke at a large Catholic high school in the Midwest, a well-dressed senior named Paul walked up to me. A sparkle lit his eye and determination showed in his step. As he held out his hand to shake mine, he said, "I want the torch."

I asked what he meant, and he explained, "I want you to pass the torch on to me, because I want to do what you're doing in this school. Though I've only got six months left here, I want to pick up where you left off."

In order to reach his goal of challenging teens to choose right over wrong, Paul expects he will have to overcome a lot of opposition from those who think "beer is king." While I was with him, he told me of three teens he knows who have family members whose lives have been ruined by alcohol. Yet his town still believes that drinking is not as dangerous as drugs, and no one calls the cops when teens have a drinking party.

Paul did not have an easy task ahead of him, but when I left, he was planning ways to gain support for his ideas. He had started to identify other students, teachers, and parents who could help him reach his goal.

At Paul's school, I pointed out that Jesus is often pictured on the cross, to remind us how much he suffered. But the good news is that he is no longer on the cross. God's Son died, was buried, and arose from the dead. I told the students, "He wants to come off that cross and enter your heart, but you have to ask him in."

If Paul wants to be a real leader, he will need faith in the God who is victorious over sin. Others will be watching Paul closely; it will take more than willpower to live the kind of life others will admire.

Turning to God

To stand up and be counted, you cannot be a wimp! You'll need to be able to stand up confidently, and you can do that if you depend on God.

Contrary to many stereotypes, people who believe in God are not wimps. God describes them in Proverbs 28:1: "The wicked flee when no one is chasing them! But the godly are bold as lions!"

Standing out requires that you be bold, courageous, and full of wisdom and strength. You can only get those qualities from God. Turning to him turns Christians into strong people, not sissies.

I've identified eight tools you'll need in your toolbox if you want to walk close to God—tools that will help you become the kind of leader Jesus will be proud of.

Tool #1. Become a child of God. Knowing God starts with accepting Jesus as your Lord and Savior. That means you'll have to have the faith and tell others of it.

> For if you tell others with your own mouth that Jesus Christ is your Lord, and believe in your own heart that God has raised him from the dead, you will be saved.
>
> Romans 10:9

Belief cannot be separated from standing out. You can't be a silent witness for Jesus.

Only God's children are led by him. But having such a valuable leader is worth standing up for. He can give you so much you'll never find anywhere else. Don't settle for the world's puny prizes when the Creator of the universe could be your light, your power, your resource, your courage, and your purpose for living.

Tool #2. Immerse yourself in God's Book. Gain wisdom by reading God's Word. Once you know him, you will need input that shows what God wants for your life. You gain that by reading the Bible—his word to you. Knowing him, you have a new heart and a new mind. Fill that mind with God's good things.

> Don't copy the behavior and customs of this world, but be a new and different person with a fresh newness

in all you do and think. Then you will learn from your own experience how his ways will really satisfy you.

Romans 12:2

Your mind needs to become filled with God's thoughts. Then you will have wisdom. When God agreed to grant Solomon's foremost desire, the Israelite king asked for wisdom. Because his heart was right, and

Don't settle for the world's puny prizes when the Creator of the universe could be your light, your power, your resource, your courage, and your purpose for living.

he had not asked selfishly, God also gave Solomon fame and prosperity.

Renew your mind over and over again with his truths by reading God's Word. See life from his point of view, not merely man's view.

When I visited Russia to hand out Bibles, I met an unforgettable woman who had learned the importance of God's truth. She was about seventy years old and told us, through a translator, that she had spent five years in a concentration camp because she would not give up her Bible.

"If you give it up and get rid of it, we will leave you alone," the authorities promised. But the Word of God was so precious to her that she held onto her Bible tightly. She lost her freedom—and nearly paid with her life—because she stood up for God's Book.

"But being with the Lord and having that book was a victory," she told us enthusiastically—a victory over Communism, oppression, and atheism. "I never gave up on God's Word, and he never gave up on me!" she exclaimed.

To be a courageous leader, you have to regularly fill your heart, mind, and soul with God's Word. That means you have to read and think about God's truth, even if it means giving up some small freedoms—like a few extra minutes of sleep!

Tool #3. Put God's Word into practice every day. It's not enough to read and study the Bible; you must put it to work! God's Word is not like those candles you see in windows during the Christmas season; they do not provide light for vision or direction. The Bible is more like a turn signal on a car or a camper's flashlight—it's meant to be *used*.

Your words are a flashlight to light the path ahead of me and keep me from stumbling.

Psalm 119:105

Do not only read God's Word; put it to use. Ask yourself as you read:

- How should this passage change my life?
- Is there a command I should obey?
- Is there wisdom I should follow?
- Does it offer direction for today? This week? This month?
- In what specific way must I use these words?

Tool #4. Act on God's promptings to your heart. When God speaks to your heart, you don't hear it with your ears—though he could do it that way if he wanted. He lets your heart know, through your conscience, that you should do something, say something, or go somewhere. When he speaks to your heart and challenges you, listen. If you turn him down, you may regret it for the rest of your life.

For if you keep on following [your old sinful nature] you are lost and will perish, but if through the power of the Holy Spirit you crush it and its evil deeds, you shall live.

Romans 8:13

God speaks to us through his Holy Spirit. Listen to what he tells you, act on it, and you can avoid much pain—and receive many blessings.

When you know that something is wrong, don't walk away from it—run! When you feel God prompting your spirit, or when he sends you a message through his Word, listen up!

Tool #5. Learn to listen. Everyone knows at least one person who can't listen—they're too busy talking! Such a person will frequently interrupt others and monopolize conversations.

A leader, however, will develop a talent for listening, and will also learn to ask questions of others—and to listen carefully to the answers.

> A fool thinks he needs no advice, but a wise man listens to others.
>
> Proverbs 12:15

As I said before, God will often speak to your heart through the Holy Spirit and his Word, but he will also lead you through human voices—if you're listening.

Tool #6. Be more concerned about God's reputation than your own pleasure. You can't separate loving God from obeying him.

> The one who obeys me is the one who loves me; and because he loves me, my Father will love him; and I will too, and I will reveal myself to him.
>
> John 14:21

Before you take action, ask yourself two questions: Would I want to have this written up in today's paper? Will it make God happy? If you can answer yes to both, you have made the right choice.

A leader is made up of his or her actions. He is the sum total of what he thinks and does. We put our integrity on the line when we act out what we believe in our hearts. So we should do all our actions in a way that will please God.

Some people who have done what pleased themselves are dying today of AIDS, because they could not

Just as God shut the mouths of the lions who could have attacked Daniel, he will stand up for you.

give up their immorality. Others are in prison because they took what they wanted, no matter who they hurt. Pleasing yourself will have a high, unpleasant price in the end. Trying to please God will help you avoid a lot of trouble.

Tool #7. Rely on God's strength. Standing for right does not guarantee popularity. Many people will not agree with you, and you will feel the barbs of their anger.

I remember a town that became bitterly angry at me because I told them some things are right and others are wrong.

"What gives you the right to tell us what is right and wrong?" they questioned me.

The officials in another school became angry when I mentioned that I have made it through life with the help of the Creator of the universe. They did not like my faith in God. Though their reaction saddened me, I drew strength from God in the midst of opposition.

God will be with you and will strengthen you when you make that difficult stand. As you feel the sting of rejection, he will heal your hurts and give you the power to keep on going. Just stay plugged in to him!

> But he gives us more and more strength to stand against all such evil longings. As the Scripture says, God gives strength to the humble but sets himself against the proud and haughty.
>
> James 4:6

Tool #8. Replace pride with a love for the Lord. God described the lifestyle of a true leader in this verse:

> If anyone respects and fears God, he will hate evil. For wisdom hates pride, arrogance, corruption and deceit of every kind.
>
> Proverbs 8:13

I'd like to share a simple, two-step leadership formula based on that verse.

• Hate what is evil. That's a way of saying, "Do what God wants you to do." You will become a true leader when you love what he loves and hate what he hates. To do that, you will have to read your Bible and know what God calls pride, arrogance, corruption, and deceit. Only reading his Word can provide you with the answers you need.

• Get rid of pride. Most teens are seeking popularity. They want to look good to others. Maybe that's natural.

But God says we should not focus on ourselves, but should forget ourselves in serving others. That's supernatural.

Ask yourself the following questions:

- Do I like to be listened to more than I listen to others?
- Do I want others to serve me—and resent serving them?

- Would I rather talk than sit quietly?
- When someone else acts like a know-it-all, do I get angry?

If you answered yes to these, Satan has convinced you that you are nothing unless you are noticed. You have bought the lie that you have to be perfect, that you have to do things for the applause of others, or you will not be a worthwhile person. He's hit you in your self-esteem while you probably weren't even looking.

Take your spiritual-pride temperature by asking yourself, Do I feel as proud when I am praying as when I talk to other people? To put it another way, Praying or preaching, which makes me feel better about myself? If you feel comfortable praying quietly inside yourself—not getting all the attention—your heart is right with God.

I confess that I would rather preach than pray, because I like the applause of the crowd. I love standing ovations and signing my books, because those things make me feel like a big shot.

But when I take the credit that way, I lose my eternal reward. Once the moment of applause is over, that's it. I've done it for people, and they have rewarded me. I've shortchanged myself because I haven't given God the credit.

But it is God who is behind my ability to write the books and give the speeches. He has given me the skills I need and allows me to live in a country where I can exercise them.

Daring Leadership

Hate the evil way of pride and you will avoid much pain. Do things God's way, and strength, courage, and wisdom will fill you. Boldness will enable you to stand against the evil world. When people say, "I don't like what you are doing," you'll be able to hold fast to your faith and turn down temptations that would separate you from God.

The prophet Daniel stood out from the crowd, though he was parted from his family and heritage. Denied his religious protection and tempted to eat foods that God had told the Israelites to avoid, he still stood fast. Daniel's conquerors even gave him the name of a pagan god. But no matter how the world fought him, the prophet stood firm. Despite the fact that friends turned their backs on him when he was thrown in the lions' den, Daniel stood out for God.

That's the kind of leader I hope you will be. Just as God shut the mouths of the lions who could have attacked Daniel, he will stand up for you. Stand out for him today!

CHECKPOINTS ✔

1. Have you ever felt as if Christians were wimps? Why? Is that stereotype really true? Why or why not?

   _____

   _____

   _____

2. Where does your strength come from? Why is it important to depend on God? Do you know him as your Savior? If not, ask him into your

heart today. If you do know him, are you living a life committed to him? Look back at the prayer for salvation at the end of chapter four. If you haven't committed your life totally to God, do it now. If you have asked Jesus to take over and are still not doing all you could for him, pray this prayer of further commitment to his work. "Dear Lord, I know I'm saved. I am walking with you but I want to run with and for you. I need you to help me to be more bold in my witness and life. Help me never be ashamed of you and to speak out for you. With your help, I know I can be all you made me to be. I love you, Lord. Amen."

_____

_____

_____

3. How can you draw closer to God? List some ways mentioned in this chapter. Are you using them daily in your walk with him? If you need to improve, what area should you target? Pray about ways you can improve your walk with God. Then put them into action.

_____

_____

_____

No Perfect Leaders

We've studied leaders from many different angles by looking at the inside stuff it takes to lead, the people who make leadership possible, and the lifestyle it entails.

But we haven't really taken a look at what makes leaders fail.

No leader (except Jesus) is perfect. Everyone who has led, throughout history, has had flaws and made mistakes. Many leaders have failed—and failed big time!

Failure is a part of life, so we need to know how to evaluate our wrongs and bounce back from them.

Where Did I Go Wrong?

Every day in the newspaper we can read of successful people from all walks of life who have fallen from power, glory, and respect. Integrity is a key part of keeping your success once you get it. Without honesty as your *only* way the fall from fame is swift and painful.

Get ideas from people who have been where you plan to go.

Leaders hold a great deal of responsibility in their hands, and much is expected of them.

For example, think in terms of your school. If you've ever been elected class president, you know that the election is the easy part. The hard part comes when you try to live out your promises. Talking leadership comes easily to most of us, but showing it to others is not as simple. That's why people will tell you that if your talk and walk are not the same, don't talk it. If you break that rule, you become a hypocrite.

Hypocrisy appears to be the number-one area of leader failure in politics. Would-be leaders promise too much and don't deliver. It's easy to promise up front, before the election, and never fulfill those promises.

In the short run, many leaders seem to get away with murder, but a person can't live that way forever. Sooner or later it's bound to catch up with them. In most cases, the next election is only four years away—and voters may not forget the unfulfilled promises.

The memories of failure can sting. Look at Judas, whom Jesus chose to be one of the twelve men who would carry the Gospel around the world. He betrayed his master with a kiss. Would you like your name to be associated with the acts of a failed leader? Look at the black name Judas has. Don't let something like this happen to you.

When you think of failed leaders, who could avoid mentioning Hitler? In a very desperate time, he gave Germany hope. Many people believed he would lead them out of economic depression and into world fame. But few knew that Hitler had his own personal agenda that included killing six million people.

Once this man had power, no one seemed able to check his evil deeds. He led by such fear and intimidation that even his generals were afraid to challenge or contradict him. Not until the end did they question him and begin to think of stopping him. Yes, Hitler led people—but in the wrong direction. Instead of using his power for right, he chose all that was evil.

Avoiding Mistakes

I know you don't want to make the mistakes that would ruin your reputation. To help you avoid goofing up (though I'm not saying you would do as badly as the men you've read about in this chapter), I've identified some checkpoints.

You can avoid much shame and pain if you keep these things in mind.

1. Stay committed to an ideal. You have to have a commitment that says, Right is right and wrong is wrong. Make your Christian principles the ruling agent in your life.

When you have this kind of commitment and someone wants you to do something wrong, hold fast to your principles. Though your determination to do right may put the election at stake, do not give in. Real leaders stick to ideals.

2. Get counsel. Advice from people who are wiser than you will keep you on track in decision making. If you wanted to climb a mountain, you would find someone who had done it before and ask him how to do it. When you face the challenge of dealing with difficult people, you will go to someone who has a lot of tact and get advice from her. She can tell you, from years of experience, what to do and what to avoid.

Make use of other people's experience; don't go it alone. Get ideas from people who have been where you plan to go. Learn from them, and you can save yourself time and energy. Experience may be the best teacher, but it is often the hardest and most painful one as well.

3. Surround yourself with people who have the same ideals. You'll want people of integrity in your corner, not those who want to lie, cheat, steal, or go against the laws of God. Lawbreakers will encourage you to share in their wrongs. So avoid teens who drink or have premarital sex, though they know it's wrong. Instead, surround yourself with those who have a commitment to obeying God's Word, upholding justice, or defending people's rights.

I'm not talking about living around human ditto marks—those who agree with all you say and never challenge you. Elvis Presley lived like that. No one ever checked him, and if someone did challenge him, Elvis fired him. Secluded and isolated from the real world, he only kept about him those who idolized him and made him into a god. No one could challenge his power.

Don't surround yourself with people who will only make you look good. You need others to help you become a better person, challenge your mistakes, or encourage you to pick what is right over the wrong. Christian leaders live humbly, not in an arrogant, prideful manner. They accept the truth from others, instead of avoiding it.

Surround yourself with people who you can look up to in faith.

4. Have well thought-out plans. If you become arrogant and full of pride, you will be diverted from your original plan to become a leader who honors God. Leaders who fail to plan are actually planning to fail. Although we do not agree with U.S. policies and Custer's attitude toward Native Americans, he is still a good example of what happens when leaders fail to plan. General George A. Custer was an experienced military leader, but his arrogance led him to make a hasty, ill-prepared attack on the Sioux and Cheyenne and it ended with the slaughter of every one of his men.

You need to plan in life, even in the little things. When I play golf and make a good practice swing, I can usually follow it up with a good shot. But if I start thinking, I hit a good shot yesterday, so I don't need to practice today, it is easy for me to goof up.

Many sports people picture what they want to do before they make the free throw or swing the bat. They have plans and review them before they go at the task. That way they are not moving into it blindly.

Think through your actions first. If you have to make a five-minute speech, don't go at it with arrogance, but with humility. Plan it, rehearse often, make it second nature to you. Then you will go into "battle" well prepared.

5. *Keep trying until you succeed.* Once you've developed a sturdy plan, put all the effort you can muster into making it work. The adage, If at first you don't succeed, try, try again, has become hackneyed, not because it's erroneous, but because good advice is repeated often.

In October 1941, while his nation was engaged in World War II, Winston Churchill was asked to speak to the students of Harrow School. He stood before the students at a time when Great Britain's survival was very much in doubt, and said:

> Never give in, never give in, never, never, never, never—in nothing, great or small, large or petty— never give in except to convictions of honor and good sense.

Work hard to complete your plans. Be prepared to revise them if you recognize a fault or discover a better way, but never give in. Keep trying until you succeed. Don't give up until you've answered these questions:

- Is my plan still workable?
- What's preventing its success?
- Can I revise it to make it better?
- Can I approach the problem from a different angle?
- Do I need to give it more time—or change course now?

- Have I done everything in my power to make it work?

Give It Your All

The goal of following God, and leading others in his way, is a large one. It's also one we can never accomplish on our own. None of us have the power and the purity to be perfect. But we can live each day for him, asking for

Becoming the leader God wants you to be doesn't take perfection, but it will take all you've got to give.

his help for every temptation and trial. Then, though we may not be perfect, we will have lives that honor him.

You can become the leader God wants you to be. It doesn't take perfection, but it will take all you've got to give—all your attention, humility, and desire—to grow in the knowledge of him and his will for you.

CHECKPOINTS ✔

1. Have you ever seen a leader fail? Perhaps it was a friend, family member, or someone else close to you. Can you identify where that person went wrong and how he or she could have avoided it?

   _____

   _____

   _____

2. Are you afraid of failing as a leader? Why or why not?

   _____

   _____

   _____

3. Review the keys to avoiding failure in leadership. Why do you think each is important? How does each keep you from failure?

   _____

   _____

   _____

Leadership
in the Balance

Would-be leaders may have many talents and God-given gifts, but unless they know how to handle their abilities, they may stand out not for their skills and qualities, but for other—not so pleasant—characteristics.

Leadership requires an often delicate balance. To help you strike that balance, I've identified some opposites you'll need to understand and keep under control.

Self-Confidence vs. Arrogance

When you walk with your head held high, believing you can face the future because of your relationship with God, you have self-confidence. Instead of worrying about your past, you believe you are capable of making decisions—and you can live with them, right or wrong.

When you are wrong, however, you can apologize, make amends (if possible), and move on. You can look people in the eye and offer them a sturdy handshake. Instead of worrying about looking foolish in front of others, you can aim at doing your best. Guilt or worries about others' opinions do not consume you.

On the other hand, if you are living by your own wisdom, letting the world determine who you are, and trying to follow the most popular fads, you have crossed the line from self-confidence into arrogance.

Basically, any skill you overuse becomes a weakness. When you walk with God in confidence, unashamed of yourself, standing up for what is right, you remain strong. It's when you hold your head so high that your nose is in the clouds, when you won't recognize others around you, and when you become too "big" to help your parents with the housework and the lawn, that you become arrogant and obnoxious. No one wants to stay around someone with that kind of pride problem.

Balance your confidence by developing a happy medium in your opinion of yourself. If you use your own positive feelings about yourself to help others learn to appreciate themselves, you will be unlikely to step over that boundary. The truly humble person has the confidence and strength to be what he is in the Lord. He can serve others without drawing attention to himself; he does that by opening a door for another, helping a friend with homework, or giving up the best seat at a play or game. Others will come first. When you can act as a servant to the people you see each day, you have true confidence.

Communicating vs. Being a Blabbermouth

Almost every leader I know is a good communicator. Real, effective leaders speak with confidence, and they speak the truth. Words are powerful tools—more powerful than we sometimes believe. The next time someone says, "A picture is worth a thousand words," suggest that they read the Gettysburg Address, the Twenty-third Psalm, or the Lord's Prayer. Real communicators know that words influence people strongly.

But a good communicator knows when words have to stop, too. Overused, the skill of communication can become deadly. A good talker must know when to stop and listen.

Have you ever known someone who talked all the time—you could never get a word in edgewise when you were with him? People don't stick around such folks for long, and they certainly won't follow their lead.

Communication requires words, but it isn't limited to them. Have you ever told someone you loved her, with your arms folded and a steely look in your eyes?

Did she believe you? Not unless her back was toward you and she couldn't hear the bitterness and anger in your voice! Your actions and tone of voice spoke louder than your words.

Or maybe you've been told, "I love you, but . . ." Like most folks, you probably couldn't remember anything before the "but." Your mind focused on the list of things the speaker felt mad about.

Do you need to improve your communication skills? Find someone to help you learn and grow in this area. Go to a few good friends, your coach, an admired teacher, or your parents and ask them to honestly answer your question, "Do I talk too much?" Then discover from them some ways you can become a better communicator.

Honest feedback from people who care for you can help shape your character, if you are willing to listen and act on good advice. It's like having a free counseling session or inviting a consultant to enter your home and share ways in which you can become more effective. Companies pay thousands of dollars to have people provide such advice for them, and you can have it for free.

But you'll need to ask, because most people will not offer their opinions. Fear that you will get angry with them will deter all but the bravest or most desperate people.

As you learn to communicate, you'll need to learn to shut your mouth sometimes. Make listening one of your skills, because you will need it often if you seek

Leadership requires an often delicate balance.

to reach out to others. Listen twice as much as you talk, and people will want to be around you. Remember, you have two ears, one mouth. Use them in that proportion. Encourage others to share their feelings, hobbies, and interests. Ask questions that make them feel good about themselves, and you will open the door to their lives.

Making Good Eye Contact vs. Being "In Your Face"

Leaders look others in the eye, instead of peering around the room, seeking something better. When you sit down with a leader, she will pay attention to you, instead of waving at twenty others who pass by.

Focusing on your companion tells him he is important. I know I'm always impressed when people look at me instead of avoiding my eye or dividing attention between me and anything else around. People who won't make eye contact don't impress others with their concern.

So make good eye contact with those who you meet. Show them that you care, but don't get too close for comfort.

An overconfident companion doesn't just look you in the face; he's in your face. You've experienced it when a stranger talks to you from six inches away. Perhaps you've started backing away or felt as if you'd like to bend over backwards to escape!

Most people feel comfortable with one-and-a-half to two feet between them and another person. Exceptions to this are a first-time meeting or someone who is very shy. Such situations may require a little more space.

Don't let your newfound confidence irritate. Keep a balance in your distance. Make a new friend feel comfortable by communicating, making eye contact, and staying just close enough to be friendly.

Serving Others vs. Neglecting Yourself

From the stories and ideas I've presented in this book, you've learned that leadership is synonymous with servanthood; it's not synonymous, however, with personal neglect.

Thinking of others, serving them, and meeting their needs is something Jesus teaches us to do. It's nearly impossible to remain depressed if you are helping someone else.

At the same time, however, don't take yourself for granted or neglect your own real needs.

I've seen church leaders lose their families because they spent every night at church. Others are so filled with false modesty and such a long guilt trip that they give all their efforts to others and leave nothing for themselves.

Don't believe that you are so unworthy of care that you must completely expend your energy on others. Instead, find a healthy balance in which you help others but keep from draining all your energies.

Some leaders forget to keep themselves in shape emotionally. The hidden pains of the past may interfere with their ability to give to others, yet they seek to pour out all their emotional resources for the good of others. When they hurt, they need to reach for help themselves—perhaps even seek counseling.

You cannot lead well if you are out of shape mentally, emotionally, physically, or spiritually. So while you are helping a pregnant woman by getting her a meal, helping your invalid neighbor by cleaning up his yard, visiting a friend in the hospital, or working with a youth ministry, keep yourself in mind, too. Don't keep moving until you are exhausted; schedule in some rest time. You have legitimate needs, too.

Reading to Broaden Your Horizons vs. Hiding in Books

Leaders read in order to learn more about life, but they don't hide in a book. Again, striking a balance is so important.

Don't read only about one subject or let your social life lapse because you just *have* to read the latest novel. Overusing your skill and neglecting other areas of your life will keep you off balance.

When you are sitting (unless you are driving a car), read. Listen to cassettes when you are on the move. Both will help you learn. But when a friend stops by, put down your book or turn off your tape. Read when you are alone; listen to others when you have the chance.

I challenge parents never to read the paper while the kids are awake. If they are in the room with Mom and Dad, kids should receive the attention they need. Dads who hide behind the paper imply that the news is more important than their children. Moms who do the crossword puzzle during playtime give their youngsters the impression that they like the paper more than the kids.

Don't read at the expense of others. Make them a part of your life, and read in the quiet moments.

Staying in Shape vs. Becoming a Fitness Freak

All of us need to stay in shape physically. If you need to get in shape, join a gym and work out. Get your heart rate to a good pace for your health. But don't become a pest about exercise and eating right. When your friends want to go out for junk food occasionally, don't spend the meal driving them crazy. Regularly harping on diet will only make them want to avoid you.

Don't get addicted to exercise flings that will not last. To see if you are on a fling, ask yourself, How long have I done it? If you have stuck with a good pattern for weeks or months, you will probably hang in there. If not, this may be a short-term fling with a new fitness program. So when you brag about it to your friends, you run the risk of making them feel bad about something that may be history in a short time.

Balance your need for exercise with the mental, emotional, and spiritual sides of your life. Physical things are important—but they are not the only thing in life.

Taking a Stand vs. Being Insensitive

When you lead others to avoid drugs, alcohol, tobacco, profanity, premarital sex, or other sins, don't be too hard on them. Though you can clearly see what's right and wrong, those you speak to may not have dealt with this area of their lives. Though they know right and wrong, they haven't personally faced their sins. Deal gently with them, and you are more likely to affect their lives.

For example, when you begin to study God's Word and walk with Jesus for a while, some sins become clear to you. As you gain an appreciation of what sin is and understand right from wrong, you alter your lifestyle.

Then a new Christian comes along who hasn't had as much time as you in the Word. If you berate her for not knowing how to find the Book of Isaiah as quickly as you do, you are wrong.

When we act insensitively, it's often because we have become proud. Putting down others because they don't know what we know about any subject means we have missed the point. Instead of recognizing that not all people have our knowledge and that we can learn from others, we have put ourselves on a pedestal.

When I train my children to work in the yard, fish, or paint a model, I need to remember that this is brand new to them. If I act as if these skills should be second nature to them and scold them for being stupid, I will discourage them. They have to start at the same level at which I started when I was a kid. It's the same in spiritual matters. We are all God's children, and we grow at different rates in different places.

Though you know bad from good, don't become insensitive to others' feelings. Love them through the learning process.

Focusing on People vs. Focusing on Projects

Certainly every leader needs to have projects and be able to stick to them. Whether it's the game you are playing this afternoon, studying for a test, exercising, or painting a room, you'll need to focus on the things you need to get done. But don't let projects push people out of your life.

You may need to work hard to accomplish your tasks, but when you please the boss with all the good you do for the company and neglect your family until your spouse leaves you, you have obviously gone too far.

People are more important than projects. Don't ever put projects ahead of a person.

For example, I am on my church basketball team. When I play, I have to remember that I'm a Christian first and foremost. If I get angry at the final point because the ref made a bad call, I show the world that having Jesus in my life means nothing. I'm no different from the people who don't have him. The project—playing to win—has become more important than the message I give to others about how the game should be played and life should be lived.

Turning the Other Cheek vs. Knowing When to Fight

Jesus told us that when someone slaps our right cheek, we need to turn the other cheek toward him. When someone asks us to walk a mile, we should walk two. If someone asks us to carry her coat, we should offer to carry her hat, too.

We should give in to the demands of the world when our humility will stand out as a testimony for God. But Jesus did not say we had to stay in the same place for years and let the same person smack our cheeks over and over. At some point common sense tells us to leave. The time may come when we need to fight for what is right.

Being Christlike does not mean we ruin ourselves by letting others take advantage of us. Just as Jesus said we should love ourselves, but did not provide specific directions on that subject, I believe he wants us to have a common-sense approach to avoid being used.

Knowing when to fight and when to flee means we must choose our battles. What is worth fighting for? What is worth walking away from? When do you tell a friend you disagree with him, and when do you hold that thought inside?

Sometimes the answer is hard to come by. In such cases, you will want to consult a wiser person. If you feel angry about something your friend said, don't act at all. Wait until you cool down. Write down what you want to say and hold on to it for six days. At the end of that time, if you still feel the same, rip up the paper and go and tell your friend. Don't leave it on paper, but speak from the heart.

Balancing Act

If you want to lead, you'll need to balance these and other areas of your life. Identify areas in which you overreact or become overcommitted and you will see the places where you need to make corrections. For example, it's great to save money for your future, but if money has become your god, you are out of balance. By looking at the attitudes that knocked you out of balance and discovering ways to change them, you can change your life for the better.

The best basis for balance is a life that puts God first, others second, and yourself third.

Balance is important to leadership because it shows people our lives are not one-sided, that they are under control, and that they take the most important things into account. People who are out of control cannot expect others to look up to them and want to have lifestyles like theirs. Who wants to be out of control and suffer the pain that kind of life brings?

The best basis for balance is a life that puts God first, others second, and yourself third. Along the way, don't forget to take care of your family and yourself. When God is in charge of your life, you will want to serve others and see that they have the best. Though you will not neglect the things you need, they will not keep you from being an effective witness for Jesus.

A life with that kind of order to it will result in a happy, content person. A person like that can become a great leader because others will want to experience such blessings!

CHECKPOINTS ✔

1. Have you known someone who had many gifts but became obnoxious? Why did that person offend you?

   _____

   _____

   _____

2. List the areas in which leaders need to develop balance. Have you struggled with any of these? Why? What have you done about it?

    _____

    _____

    _____

3. Do you need to gain balance in some areas you've never really thought about? List a few, along with ideas about how you can get balanced. (If you need help, ask a friend, youth counselor, parent, or other person who can give you advice.)

    _____

    _____

    _____

4. What are the priorities that result in a happy, content person? Are they part of your life? Do you need to change some priorities?

    _____

    _____

    _____

You're a Leader!

Standing out in a crowd because you're standing up for a cause—that's what this book has been about. How about you? Do you feel better equipped to make your mark in a world that desperately needs to be touched with the Good News?

I want you to make a difference in your world. I know you can be a leader because I believe in a miracle-working and difference-making God. If God could change me from a shy, self-centered sinner to a man of God, he can change you as well. He wants to hold you in his loving arms when you are hurting and be your source of energy when you are lazy and don't feel like pleasing him. Let him fill you each day with life-sustaining courage by filling your mind and heart with his words and wisdom. Talk to him and go to him before every decision you make—big or small. Lean on him and share him with others. If you will STAND OUT for Jesus, he'll see to it that you have the strength to stand out for the purposes he has placed in you. Here are some tips to remind you how you can keep growing as a leader.

1. *Read your Bible daily.* If you miss a day it's no big deal. Pick it up the next day.
2. *Read great books.* Read biographies. Learn how other great achievers set their goals and stuck to their vision of standing out for a cause.
3. *Talk to older, wiser people.* Make it a habit to listen when wiser people share their ideas. Shut up and learn. Don't miss daily opportunities to stretch your imagination.
4. *Get the right amount of rest for you.* If you are tired and fatigued you'll never stand out. It's hard to stand up when you aren't refreshed.
5. *Exercise at least four times a week.* It doesn't matter what kind of exercise is best for you. Find it—then do it!
6. *Treat others with respect.* It doesn't matter if they are younger or if you feel they don't deserve it. It's the right thing to do. You will benefit greatly from this daily discipline.
7. *In all areas of your life ask: Is this in or out of balance?* A balanced life is a gift from God. Don't be so overboard on any one area that it runs your life. Use your common sense. Stay balanced. If you don't know if you are going overboard on something, ask your friends. They'll tell you.
8. *Be willing to take criticism.* It's the only way to grow. Be big enough to take it—from anyone or anywhere.
9. *Be kind and gentle.* Practice kindness with young children, animals—everything. What you give out will come back. You'll also sleep better.

10. *Work hard at everything you do.* Actually you are doing it for God and not others, so do it well. Give everything your best shot.
11. *Be willing to take risks.* If anything is worth doing, it's worth taking the chance of doing it wrong. Someday you'll be glad you took the risk, because the learning experience will help you grow.
12. *Don't judge others.* Walk in their shoes before you think you know why they do the things they do.
13. *Never gossip.* If you are so small that you tear others down behind their backs, you'll never stand out for God.
14. *Love others.* Live by the golden rule. Give out what you want back. Be Christlike in everything you do and say.
15. *Be likable and not disagreeable.* Build other people's ideas up. Encourage people to talk about what's important to them.
16. *Serve others.* That's what leadership is all about. Jesus came from glory to wash feet and die for our sins. The least we can do is help around the house. Stand out among your family and you'll much more easily stand out in the world.

The time is at hand to put this book into practice. Go back and look over the pages that inspired you, touched your heart, or challenged you to action when you first read them. Put them on index cards and stick them as reminders in your room, locker, or any place you'll see them often. As you go through your day, ask yourself, What do I want to be remembered for in my life? Start on it today. Be true to your dreams and hopes and aspirations. Be relentless in your pursuit of greatness for God. Never stop trying to reach your star. God has it waiting with your name on it and only requires that you put in the effort to grab hold of it. He will be your inspiration if you'll take the time to talk to him and let him talk to you. Remember that with God as your guide, you *can* be a leader!

If this book has touched your life, if you need to share a joy or a pain, if you would like a list of my other books and cassettes, or if you want to know how to bring me to speak to your school or group, write me at this address:

BILL SANDERS
P.O. Box 711
Portage, Michigan 49081